MORE
Herrschners®
Blue-Ribbon
Afghans

More Herrschners Blue-Ribbon Afghans

Trina Laube-Oltmann
Creative Director, *Blue-Ribbon Afghans*

Gloriann Doyle
Editorial Manager

Jennifer Mitchell
Project Editor

Communication Logistics, Inc.
Creative Services/Project Photography

Leisure Arts
Cover Photography

Linda Bentz, Peggy Yates
Technical Advisors

Maureen Ruth
Vice President, Publishing

Printed in the United States of America. First Printing.
ISBN: 1-60140-322-4

INTRODUCTION

Page 20

Herrschners® Grand National Afghan Competition has challenged and inspired knitters and crocheters *across America* to design some truly magnificent afghans. Since 1991, the competition has offered categories in crocheted, knit, baby, juvenile, and embroidered afghans. There is something for everyone! We've gathered some of the *top designs* that caught the judges' eyes. This collection of award-winning afghans will inspire and challenge you as well!

Page 34

Page 58

You'll discover projects *as fun to knit and crochet as they are to admire.* Offering everything from basic stitches to advanced techniques and color changes, you'll enjoy these amazing afghans every stitch of the way! And the best part is once you have completed one you not only have a lovely *home accent piece,* you also have a beautiful throw to *keep you warm* on chilly nights!

Do you prefer softer, muted shades? Bright and bold designs? We have the pattern for you! Do you enjoy working in squares, so you can take your stitching with you wherever you go? You'll find that, too! Searching for a *great gift* or a perfect accent for your three-seasons porch? Look no further! Whatever your style, you'll find an afghan (or two, three, or four!) you just can't wait to create.

Page 102

Go ahead—choose one of these diverse designs, grab your needles or hook and some yarn, and *start stitching a **winning creation** of your own!*

Page 68

Page 12

Page 30

MORE
Herrschners
Blue-Ribbon **Afghans**

Contents

Whatever your style,

you'll find something to

warm your heart and your

home in this collection of

award-winning knit and

crocheted afghans.

Crocheted Afghans
FOR EVERY SEASON

Keepsake Afghans
FOR BABY

Page 50

Page 82

Page 94

Knit Afghans
FOR ANY HOME

Embroidered Afghans
FOR COMFORT & STYLE

Amazing Afghans
FOR COOL KIDS

The Basics
FOR KNIT & CROCHET

Tropical Delight Afghan
Instructions begin on page 8.

Crocheted Afghans
FOR EVERY SEASON

Draped over your lap, used as a beautiful bedspread, or folded on the back of your sofa—however you choose to use these crocheted creations, you will find delight in them throughout the year.

The soft shades of "Eve's Coverlet" and "Tropical Delight," and the blooming squares of "Floral Bouquet" are a lovely reminder of warm, sunny days. "First Snowfall" stirs up memories of snow angels, chilly days by a warm fire, and your favorite sledding hill. The "Harlequin" afghan's vibrant colors make it stand out in an autumn display and bring smiles year-round, while the "Double Wedding Ring" afghan makes a perfect present during the season of love.

Present these dazzling designs as a collection of afghans created from the heart, or bring a new one out each time the season changes. Whether sunny or snowy, windy or warm, you will enjoy crocheting these afghans as much as using them.

Tropical Delight

Featuring a basic granny-square design embellished with a unique popcorn stitch, this colorful afghan will warm your heart and your home. Cuddle up with it on a chilly winter afternoon and dream about a tropical-island getaway.

Design by Susan Stevens of Eastlake, Ohio

MATERIALS

2 FINE

- **3-ply sport weight yarn**
  - -White (21 oz, 1,782 yds)
  - -Light Yellow (14 oz, 1,188 yds)
  - -Mint (14 oz, 1,188 yds)
  - -Pink (14 oz, 1,188 yds)
  - -Sky Blue (14 oz, 1,188 yds)
- **Crochet hook,**
  size F-5 (3.75 mm)
  or size to obtain gauge
- **Tapestry needle**

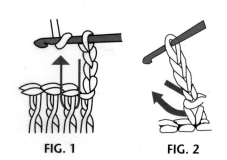

FIG. 1   **FIG. 2**

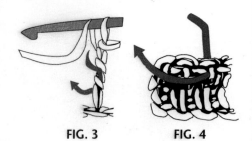

FIG. 3   **FIG. 4**

AFGHAN FINISHED SIZE
Approx 39" × 53"

AFGHAN GAUGE
One square = 7" × 7"

Note: Be sure to check the size of the finished square. The square is worked tightly. If the square is too large, it will spoil the desired look and you will have insufficient yarn.

STITCH GUIDE

Tr tr (triple treble): Yo hook 4 times, insert hook into st, yo and pull up lp, yo and draw through 2 lps at a time until only 1 lp remains on hook.

FPSlst (front post slip stitch): Sl st around top of pc.

FPsc (front post single crochet): Sc around top of pc.

FPdc (front post double crochet): Dc around top of pc or around post of specified st (Fig. 1).

FPtr (front post treble crochet): Tr around post of specified st.

Shaped Popcorns Note: *Work multiple sts in first sc, as in Fig. 2 or into base of first tr, as in Fig. 3. Then remove hook and insert into both lps of specified st. Catch lp of last st worked and pull through. Pc made.*

beg-sh-pc (beginning shaped popcorn): Sc, ch 3 into st or ring specified. 3 dc into sc, as in Fig. 3. Remove hook, insert into third ch worked, finish pc.

sh-pc-A (shaped popcorn A): Tr into st or ring specified. 3 dc into base of tr, as in Fig. 3. Remove hook, insert into both lps of first tr worked (Fig. 4), finish pc.

sh-pc-B (shaped popcorn B): Tr into st specified. 2 dc, ch 1 into base of tr, as shown in Fig. 3. Remove hook, insert hook into both lps of first tr worked (Fig. 4), finish pc.

sh-pc-C (shaped popcorn C): Tr into st specified. 2 dc into base of tr as shown in Fig. 3. Remove hook, insert hook into fourth ch of ch-4 worked just before beg tr (Fig. 4), finish pc.

Note: Around beg sc: ch 1, OR ch 1, sc; the ch-1 always counts as a dc. These sts mimic the post of a double crochet. When the end of a rnd is joined, always join as specified for that rnd into the next (second) dc for invisible joining.

hdc (half double crochet): Yo and insert hook where indicated, catch yarn and draw a lp through the ch (3 lps on hook), yo and draw a lp through all 3 lps to complete st.

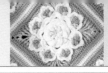

FIG. 5

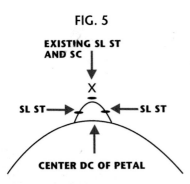

EXISTING SL ST
AND SC

SL ST →   ← SL ST

CENTER DC OF PETAL

Fig. 5: Work in front of petal in the same dc as two previous rnds. Insert hook behind st, come to front in center of st. Yo, pull through lp on hook, Sl st made. Insert hook back through center of st again. Come to front, left of st. Yo, pull through lp on hook, Sl st made.

DIRECTIONS

SQUARES (MAKE 35)

With Light Yellow, ch 4, join with Sl st to first ch to form a ring.

■ **Rnd 1:** Work beg-sh-pc in ring, ch 3, (sh-pc-A in ring, ch 3) 7 times. Join with Sl st in third ch of beg pc. (8 pc) Fasten off leaving a 4" tail for weaving.

■ **Rnd 2:** *Note: Rnd 2 contains 8 overlapping petals, each worked across 3 sps.*
Petal 1: With White, join with Sl st in any ch-3 sp, ch 5, turn work to WS. (Sl st, ch 3) in next ch-3 sp *(note: ch 3 doesn't count as dc).* Turn work to RS. Work 10 dc in ch-5 sp, ch 1. Sl st in next ch-3 sp.
Petals 2-6: Ch 5, turn work to WS, Sl st to the left of previous Sl st in next ch-3 sp, ch 3, turn work to RS. Work 10 dc in ch-5 sp, ch 1, Sl st in next ch-3 sp.
Petal 7: Ch 5, turn work to WS. Sl st to the left of previous Sl st in next ch-3 sp, ch 3, turn work to RS. Work 10 dc in ch-5 sp, ch 1. Working in front of first petal made, Sl st to the left of Sl st in next ch-3 sp.
Petal 8: Ch 5, turn work to WS, Sl st to the left of Sl st in next ch-3 sp, ch 3, turn work to RS. Work 10 dc in ch-5 sp, ch 1. Working in front of first petal made, Sl st into post of first Sl st of second petal made.

■ **Rnd 3:** Pull eighth petal forward. Working to the right (backward), ch 3, Sl st around base of ch-3 of first petal made. Ch 3, return petal to normal position, Sl st in BLO of sixth dc (fifth from the left) of eighth petal made.
Note: The ch-3 at beg of each petal doesn't count as a dc.
(Ch 7, Sl st in first dc of same petal. Ch 5, Sl st in BLO of sixth dc in next petal) 7 times, ch 7, Sl st in first dc of same petal, ch 5, Sl st in beg Sl st of Petal 8.

■ **Rnd 4:** Sc over joining Sl st. Work in front of and sk ch-7 lps between petals. [(Sc, 9 dc, sc) in next ch-5 sp] 8 times. Join with Sl st in first sc made.

■ **Rnd 5:** Sl st in sp between the 2 sc, sk sc, Sl st in each 9 dc, and in each sc around. Join with Sl st in first Sl st made as in Fig. 6. Fasten off.

■ **Rnd 6:** *Note: Ignore all Sl sts of Rnd 5. Only work into middle (fifth) dc of each Rnd-4 petal and into center (fourth) ch of skipped ch-7 lps (same sts are used on Rnds 7 and 8).* With Mint, (Sl st in BLO of middle dc of petal, ch 2, sh-pc-B in center ch of ch-7 lp. Ch 3, Sl st in same center ch of ch-7 lp. Ch 4, sh-pc-C in same center ch of ch-7 lp, ch 2) 8 times. Join with Sl st in first Sl st made. Fasten off.

■ **Rnd 7:** *Note: Work over Sl sts of Rnd 6.* With Pink and slipknot on hook, (sc in center dc of petal, ch 2, FPSlst tightly around top of next pc, ch 2, sh-pc-A into center ch of ch-7 lp, ch 3, sh-pc-A into same center ch of ch-7 lp, ch 2, FPSlst tightly around top of next pc, ch 2) 8 times. Join with Sl st in first sc made. Fasten off.

■ **Rnd 8:** With White and slipknot on hook, [work 2 Sl sts into center dc of Rnd-4 petal, as in Fig. 5. Ch 1, FPdc around top of next pc in front of and hiding Rnd-7 FPSlst, 5 dc in next ch-2 sp, FPsc around top of next pc, (3 dc, ch 1, 3 dc) in next ch-3 sp (center shell made), FPsc around next pc, 5 dc in next ch-2 sp, FPdc around next pc, ch 1] 8 times. Cut yarn. Fasten off and join in first Sl st made, as in Fig. 6.

■ **Rnd 9:** *Note: Work behind Rnd 8 down into Rnd 7. Use sp between sts to work around the ch-2 sps in Rnd 7.* With Mint and slipknot on hook, [sc into sp between FPsc

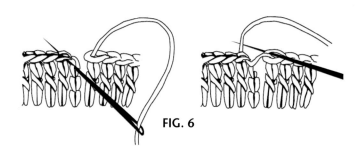

FIG. 6

and dc just after Rnd-8 center shell, ch 2, sk next 5 dc and FPdc, dc in Rnd-7 sc (hidden behind next 2 Sl sts), ch 2, sk ch-1, FPdc and 5 dc, sc in sp before next FPsc, ch 2, dc after next FPsc, ch 2, (3 Tr tr, ch 3, 3 Tr tr, ch 2) in next Rnd-7 sc, dc before next FPsc, ch 2] around. Join with Sl st in first sc made.

- **Rnd 10:** (Ch 1, sc, ch 1) in same st as joining, [2 dc in next ch-2 sp, dc in next dc, 2 dc in next ch-2 sp, (dc in next st, dc in next sp) twice, (FPtr around next Tr tr, dc in sp between Tr tr) twice, FPtr around next Tr tr, (2 dc, ch 2, 2 dc) in corner sp, (FPtr around next Tr tr, dc in next sp) 3 times, dc in next dc, dc in next sp, dc in next sc] around but omit dc at end of last rep. Cut yarn. Fasten off and join in first st, as in Fig. 6. (27 sts along each side, not counting corner chs)

- **Rnd 11:** With Sky Blue and slipknot on hook, sc in last dc of any side of square (just before corner chs), ch 1, * (2 dc, ch 2, 2 dc) in corner sp, sk 1 dc, dc in next dc, dc in next tr, FPdc around same tr, dc in next dc, (FPdc around next tr, dc in next dc) twice. The next dc is worked through 2 sts at once. Yo and slip hook through BLO of ch in Rnd-8 center shell and then through BLO of next dc, pull lp through both sts and finish dc. Dc in next 9 dc. Dc through both sts as before. (Dc in next dc, FPdc around next tr) 3 times, dc in next 2 dc; rep from * around, omitting dc at end of last rep. Join with Sl st to second dc made. (31 sts along each side)

- **Rnd 12:** Sl st in each st around, working 2 Sl sts inside sps at corners. Cut yarn. Fasten off and join in first Sl st made, as in Fig. 6.

- **Rnd 13:** *Note: Ignore all Rnd-12 Sl sts. Work in Rnd-11 dcs.* With Pink and slipknot on hook, sc in next-to-last dc of any side (counts as hdc). Hdc in next dc, (2 hdc, ch 2, 2 hdc over both chs of corner, sk first dc of next side, hdc in each dc across to corner) rep around. Cut yarn. Fasten off and join in second hdc made, as in Fig. 6. (34 hdc along each side)

- **Rnd 14:** With Light Yellow and slipknot on hook, sc in next-to-last hdc of any side (counts as hdc),

* (2 hdc, ch 2, 2 hdc) in corner sp, sk first hdc of next side, working in BLO, hdc in each hdc across to corner, rep from * around. Cut yarn. Fasten off and join in second hdc made, as in Fig. 6. (37 hdc along each side)

JOINING SQUARES

Lay 2 squares side by side with RS facing up. Always begin in the right square and end in the left square, keeping the yarn between both squares. Always work sts with the hook going from the front to the back through both lps of hdcs and through corner ch-sps from front to back. With slipknot on hook, Sl st in corner sp of right square, Sl st in corner sp of left square, ch 3, 3 dc into first ch of ch-3, remove hook, insert hook into third ch, catch lp of last st worked and pull through (joining pc made). Sl st in first hdc of right square, Sl st in second hdc of left square, Sl st in each hdc continuing to alternate from right to left square to corner. Work joining pc as above. Sl st in right square corner sp, Sl st in left square corner sp. Do not cut yarn. Add 2 more squares and rep same joining process until 2 rows of 5 squares are joined. Add squares until 7 rows are attached. Rep joining process to join the rest of the squares. Work in front of existing join at corners. Fasten off.

Sl st Rnd: With Light Yellow, join with Sl st in last hdc before any corner of afghan, (Sl st into next 2 corner chs, * Sl st in each hdc of next side across to square joining, sc in next sp, FPsc around top of next pc, sc in next sp; rep from * across to next corner) rep around.

BORDER

- **Rnd 1:** *Note: Ignore last Sl st Rnd of afghan. Work in top of hdc from Rnd 14 of each square. There should be a Sl st worked in the last hdc before and in the second hdc after each square joining and each corner sp.* With White, beg at left of afghan corner, Sl st in last hdc to the right of first square joining, ch 5, (* sk next 4 sts, Sl st in next

TIP

Are you left-handed? Patterns for projects most often appear with instructions for right-handers only, so it may be worthwhile to learn these techniques. Since yarn work is shared between the hands, you may find it surprisingly easy for you to use the accompanying diagrams. If working in this way is not comfortable, use a mirror to reverse the diagrams or reverse them on a photocopier.

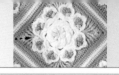

hdc, ch 5; rep from * across to corner. Sk next 2 corner chs and first hdc. Sl st in second hdc of next side) rep around.

■ **Rnd 2:** Ch 1, sc, ch 1, 9 dc in next ch-5 sp. Sk next ch-5, keeping skipped ch-5 behind work. Sl st down into third hdc of last hdc rnd of afghan. (* 11 dc in next ch-5 sp, sk next ch-5 sp, Sl st down into third hdc; rep from * across to corner, 13 dc in corner sp, sk next ch-5 sp, Sl st down in third hdc) rep around to first petal made. Finish first petal with dc worked over beg ch-1. Sk next sc and ch-1, join with Sl st to next dc.

■ **Rnd 3:** (Sl st in each dc of petal, Sl st over next Sl st down into same hdc Sl st was worked into from previous rnd) rep around. Cut yarn. Fasten off and join, as in Fig. 6.

■ **Rnd 4:** *Note: Ignore all Sl sts of Rnd 3. Work only in center dc of each petal and center ch of skipped ch-5 lp. Also only work into designated dcs of corner 13 dc.* With Mint and slipknot on hook, [(Sl st in BLO of middle (sixth) dc of petal, ch 2, * sh-pc-B in center ch of skipped ch-5 lp. Ch 3, Sl st in same center ch of ch-5 lp. Ch 4, sh-pc-C in same center ch of ch-5 lp, ch 2 **) across to corner. Sl st in fourth dc of corner petal, ch 2. Work from * to ** one time in center (seventh) dc of corner petal instead of ch-5 lp. Sl st in tenth dc of corner, ch 2. Rep from * to ** in center ch of next ch-5 lp] rep around.

■ **Rnd 5:** With Pink and slipknot on hook, work over Sl sts of Rnd 4. [* Sc in center (sixth) dc of petal, ch 2, FPSlst tightly around top of next pc. Ch 2, sh-pc-A in center (third) ch of ch-5 lp, ch 3, sh-pc-A into same center ch of ch-5 lp, ch 2. FPSlst tightly around top of next pc, ch 2; rep from * across to next corner. Work same pattern into center dc of corner petal instead of ch-5 lp] rep around. Join with Sl st in first sc made. Fasten off.

■ **Rnd 6:** With White and slipknot on hook, [work 2 Sl sts to center dc of White petal, as in Fig. 5. Ch 1, FPdc around top of next pc, 5 dc in next ch-2 sp, FPsc around top of next pc. (3 dc, ch 1, 3 dc) in next ch-3 sp, center shell made, FPsc around top of next pc, 5 dc in next ch-2 sp, FPdc around top of next pc] rep around. Join with Sl st to first Sl st made. Fasten off.

■ **Rnd 7:** *Note: Work behind Rnd 6 down into Rnd 5. Use same methods as used on Rnd 9 of square.* With Mint and slipknot on hook, [sc into sp between FPsc and dc (just after Rnd-6 center shell), ch 2, sk next 5 dc and FPdc, dc in Rnd-5 sc (hidden behind next 2 Sl sts), ch 2.

Sk ch 1, FPdc, and 5 dc. Sc in sp before next FPsc, ch 2 across to corner, ch 4 instead of ch 2 behind corner center shell] rep around. Join with Sl st in first sc made.

■ **Rnd 8:** (Ch 1, sc, ch 1) in same sc as joining [* (2 dc in next ch-2 sp, dc in next dc, 2 dc in next ch-2 sp, dc in next sc**, 3 dc in next ch-2 sp behind center shell, dc in next sc) rep across to corner ending with * to ** before corner center petal, work 9 dc in corner center petal ch-4 sp, dc in next sc] rep around. Cut yarn. Fasten off and join as in Fig. 6.

■ **Rnd 9:** Working behind any center shell of side, with Sky Blue and slipknot on hook, sc in last dc before the 3 dc behind center shell, ch-1, dc in next dc, (* work in BLO through 2 sts at once in center ch-1 of center shell and through BLO of next dc, dc in next 9 dc **; rep from * to ** across to corner 9 dc, 2 dc in next dc, dc in next 2 dc, 2 dc in next dc, work dc through BLO of ch-1 of center shell and BLO of next dc, 2 dc in next dc, dc in next 2 dc, 2 dc in next dc, dc across to next center dc of 3 dc behind next center shell) rep around. Sk first sc and first ch-1 made, Sl st in next dc.

■ **Rnd 10:** Sl st in each dc around. Cut yarn. Fasten off and join as in Fig. 6.

■ **Rnd 11:** *Note: Ignore all Rnd-10 sts. Work into Rnd-9 dcs.* With Pink and slipknot on hook, sc in any dc (counts as hdc), hdc in each dc around. Cut yarn. Fasten off and join as in Fig. 6.

■ **Rnd 12:** With Light Yellow and slipknot on hook, and working into BLO of each hdc, (Sl st, ch 2, hdc) in center hdc of a corner, [sk next hdc (Sl st, ch 2, hdc) in next hdc] rep around. Cut yarn. Fasten off and join as in Fig. 6. ❖

First Snowfall

Capture the uniqueness and wonder of the first snowfall with this wonderful winter design. The glitter yarn adds extra sparkle to the crocheted snowflakes. You'll receive a flurry of compliments as you display it throughout the winter months!

Design by Anita Moore of Calabash, North Carolina

MATERIALS

- **4-ply worsted weight yarn**
  -Light Blue (72 oz, 3,744 yds)
  -White Glitter (24 oz, 1,269 yds)
- **Crochet hooks, size F-5 (3.75 mm) and size H-8 (5.0 mm) or sizes to obtain gauge**
- **Tapestry needle**

AFGHAN FINISHED SIZE
Approx 55" × 67"

AFGHAN GAUGE
Octagon = 10¼" tall × 10¼" wide

STITCH GUIDE

sc2tog (single crochet 2 stitches together): Draw a lp through each of the next 2 sts, yo, draw the yarn through all 3 lps on the hook. One st has been made from the 2 sts.

dc2tog (double crochet 2 stitches together): Yo, insert hook in st, draw up a lp, yo, draw through 2 lps, yo, insert hook in next st, draw up a lp, yo, draw through 2 lps (3 lps on hook), yo, draw through rem 3 lps.

picot: Ch 4, Sl st in fourth ch from hook. (one picot made)

Tr (treble crochet): Yo twice, insert hook in st, draw up a lp (4 lps on hook), (Yo and draw through 2 lps) 3 times.

DIRECTIONS

SNOWFLAKE (MAKE 30)

With White Glitter and F-5 hook, ch 8, join with Sl st to form a ring.

- **Rnd 1 (RS):** Ch 4 (counts as first dc plus ch-1), (dc, ch 1) 15 times into the ring, join with Sl st to third ch of in beg ch-4. Place marker to show RS. (16 dc and 16 ch-1 sps)

- **Rnd 2:** Sl st in first ch-sp, ch 1, sc in same sp, ch 7, sk next ch-1 sp, * sc in next ch-1 sp, ch 4, Sl st in fourth ch from hook, sc in same sp (picot made), ch 7, sk next ch-1 sp; rep from * around to beg sc, sc in same sp as beg sc, picot, Sl st in beg sc. (8 lps and 8 picots)

- **Rnd 3:** Sl st in next 3 chs, ch 1, sc in same ch-7 sp, ch 10, * sk picot and sc in next ch-7 sp, ch 10; rep from * around. Join with Sl st in first Sl st. (8 lps and 8 sc)

- **Rnd 4:** Sl st in next lp, ch 1, in lp work the following (sc, picot, sc, picot, sc, ch 4, tr, ch 6, Sl st in sixth ch from hook, tr, ch 4, sc, picot, sc, picot, sc); rep in each lp around, Sl st into first sc, fasten off.

LARGE OCTAGON (MAKE 30)

With Light Blue and H-8 hook, ch 6, join with Sl st to form a ring.

- **Rnd 1 (RS):** In ring, ch 3 (counts as first dc), work 19 dc, Sl st in top of beg ch-3. Place marker to show RS. (20 dc)

- **Rnd 2:** Ch 3, dc in same st, 2 dc in each st around, Sl st in top of beg ch-3. (40 dc)
  Note: For Rows 3-7, you will be turning your work instead of working in the rnd.

- **Row 3:** Ch 1, sc in same st, sc in next 3 dc, * ch 3, sk next st, sc in next 4 dc; rep from * around, ch 3, join with Sl st in first sc, ch 3, turn. (32 sc and 8 ch-3 lps)

- **Row 4:** * Dc2tog, ch 2, dc2tog in corner ch-3 lp, dc in each st to next ch-3 corner lp; rep from * around, join with Sl st in beg ch-3, ch 3, turn. (48 dc and 8 ch-2 lps)

- **Row 5:** Dc in each st to ch-2 corner lp, * (dc2tog, ch 2, dc2tog) in corner ch-2 lp, dc in each st to next ch-2 corner lp; rep from * around, join with Sl st in starting ch-3, ch 3, turn. (64 dc and 8 ch-2 lps)

- **Row 6:** Dc in each st to ch-2 corner lp, * dc, ch 2, dc in corner ch-2 lp, dc in each st to next ch-2 corner lp; rep from * around, join with Sl st in beg ch-3, ch 3, turn. (80 dc and 8 ch-2 lps)

- **Rnd 7:** Dc in each st to ch-2 corner lp, * dc, ch 2, dc in corner ch-2 lp, dc in each st to next ch-2 corner lp; rep from * around, join with Sl st in beg ch-3, ch 1, turn. (96 dc and 8 ch-2 lps)

- **Rnd 8 (Joining Rnd):** Sc in same st, sc in each st to corner ch-2 lp, * holding snowflake and Light Blue octagon tog (WS of snowflake to RS of octagon), (sc, ch 1, sc) in corner ch-2 lp going through ch-2 sp and snowflake tip at once, sc in each st (Light Blue octagon) to next corner; rep from * around, join with Sl st to beg sc, turn. (112 sc and 8 ch-1 sps)

- **Rnd 9:** Ch 1, sc in same st, * sc in each st to corner; ch-1 sp, 2 sc in corner; rep from * around, Sl st in beg sc, fasten off. (128 sc with 16 sc on each of 8 sides)

SMALL DIAMOND (MAKE 20)
With White Glitter and F-5 hook, ch 6, join with Sl st to form a ring.

- **Rnd 1 (RS):** Ch 4 (counts as first dc and ch-1 sp), (dc, ch 1) in ring 11 times, join with Sl st to third ch in beg ch-4, do not turn. Place marker to show RS. (12 dc and 12 ch-1 sps)

- **Rnd 2:** Sl st in first ch-1 sp, ch 1, sc in same sp *, (ch 4, sc) in next ch-1 sp; rep from * in each ch-1 sp around, join with Sl st to first sc, fasten off. (12 ch-4 lps)

- **Rnd 3:** With Light Blue and H-8 hook, join with sc to any ch-4 lp, sc in same lp, ch 1, 2 sc in next ch-4 lp, ch 1, 2 sc in next ch-4 lp, ch 3, * (2 sc in next ch-4 lp, ch 1) twice, 2 sc in next ch-4 lp, ch 3; rep from * around, join with Sl st in beg sc. (24 sc, 8 ch-1 sps, 4 ch-3 sps)

- **Rnd 4:** Ch 3, * (dc in each sc, 2 dc in ch-1 sp) across to ch-3 corner, 2 dc, ch 2, 2 dc in corner; rep from * around, join with Sl st to beg dc, do not turn. (56 dc and 4 ch-2 sps)

- **Rnd 5:** Ch 1, sc in same st, * sc in each st to corner, work 2 sc in corner; rep from * 3 more times, sc in each st to beg sc, join with Sl st to first sc, fasten off. (64 sc, 16 sc on each of 4 sides)

FINISHING
Steam-block all pieces before sewing. If using an iron, take care not to touch the yarn. Hold the iron above the yarn and keep it in constant motion. Let pieces dry thoroughly. Holding right sides together and working in BLO of octagons, whipstitch octagons together in 6-octagon strips. Whipstitch strips together in BLO. Whipstitch diamonds in BLO of each diamond-shaped sp. Sew all octagons together, holding together and sewing through BLO. Afghan is 5 octagons wide and 6 octagons long. Place small diamonds in corner sps where octagons do not meet. Whipstitch through BLO.

BORDER
- **Rnd 1:** With White Glitter, H-8 hook, and working in BLO, join yarn with sc in outside corner, work 2 sc in same st, [* sc in BLO of next 15 sc, 3 sc in BLO of next

> ## TIP
> To properly store your seasonal afghan the rest of the year, follow these steps.
> - Clean and dry the afghan completely.
> - Fold it with as few folds as possible and lay it flat. Never hang the afghan when storing it.
> - Wrap the afghan in acid-free tissue or in cotton muslin that has been washed in hot water several times and thoroughly dried. Do not put the afghan in a plastic bag, as moisture can accumulate.
> - Place it in an acid-free cardboard box or in a trunk with cedar chips. Make sure the cedar chips are not in direct contact with the afghan.
> - Keep the box in a cool, dry place.

TIP

To prevent woven-in ends from coming loose, weave on a diagonal line instead of straight up or across as you may be accustomed to doing.

sc; rep from * once, sc in BLO of next 15 sc, sk 2 inside corner sts (where octagons meet), sc in BLO of next 15 sc, 3 sc in BLO of next sc] rep around adjusting for outside or inside corners, join with Sl st in beg sc, fasten off.

■ **Rnd 2:** With Light Blue and H-8 hook, join with Sl st in center outside corner sc, ch 3 (counts as first dc), (1 dc, ch 1, 2 dc) in same st, * sk next 2 sts, (2 dc, ch 1, 2 dc) in next st; rep from * to inside corner ending with 2 dc in st just before inside corner, 2 dc in second sc

from corner, ch 1; rep from * around, join with Sl st to beg dc, fasten off.

■ **Rnd 3:** With White Glitter and H-8 hook, join with sc in ch-1 sp of outside corner, ch 2, sc in same sp, [* sc in next st, sc2tog, sc in next st, sc in next ch-1 sp, ch 2, sc in same sp; rep from * to inside corner ending with sc in next st, (sc2tog) 3 times at inside corner, sc in next st, sc in next ch-1 sp, ch 2, sc in same sp] rep around afghan, join with Sl st to beg sc, fasten off. ❖

Floral Bouquet

Create the joy of spring with this gorgeous, blooming afghan. The three-dimensional flowers are alive with color. Worked in squares, the motifs are perfect for a pillow as well.

Design by Roseanna Beck of Fords, New Jersey

AFGHAN MATERIALS

- **4-ply worsted weight yarn**
  - -White (14 oz, 720 yds)
  - -Bright Light Green (10 oz, 480 yds)
  - -Light Blue (MC) (3 oz, 128 yds)
  - -Light Lavender (MC) (3 oz, 128 yds)
  - -Dark Pink (CC) (24 yds)
  - -Medium Coral (CC) (24 yds)
  - -Bright Gold (CC) (24 yds)
  - -Bright Dark Green (10 oz, 480 yds)
  - -Light Pink (MC) (3 oz, 128 yds)
  - -Light Coral (MC) (3 oz, 128 yds)
  - -Bright Yellow (MC) (3 oz, 128 yds)
  - -Dark Blue (CC) (24 yds)
  - -Lavender (CC) (24 yds)

- **Crochet hooks, size H-8 (5.0 mm) and size I-9 (5.5 mm) or sizes to obtain gauge**

- **Tapestry needle** ◼ **Sewing needle** ◼ **White sewing thread**

AFGHAN FINISHED SIZE
Approx 47" × 58"

AFGHAN GAUGE
One square = 5½" × 5½"

STITCH GUIDE
hdc (half double crochet):
Yo and insert hook where indicated, catch yarn and draw a lp through the ch (3 lps on hook), yo and draw a loop through all 3 lps to complete st.

shell: 2 dc, ch 2, 2 dc

AFGHAN DIRECTIONS

SQUARES
Make 16 squares of each of the following combinations, for a total of 80 squares:

Main Color (MC)	Contrasting Color (CC)
Light Pink	Dark Pink
Light Blue	Dark Blue
Light Coral	Medium Coral
Light Lavender	Lavender
Bright Yellow	Bright Gold

- **Rnd 1:** With H-8 hook and MC, ch 2, work 8 sc in second ch from hook, join with Sl st to beg sc.

- **Rnd 2:** For petals, (sc, 2 dc) in each sc around, join with Sl st to beg sc, fasten off.

- **Rnd 3:** Working behind petals of Rnd 1, join CC with a Sl st bet any 2 sc, sc in same sp, ch 3, * sc bet next 2 sc, ch 3; rep from * around, join to beg sc, fasten off. (8 ch-3 sps)

- **Rnd 4:** Join MC with a Sl st in any ch-3 sp, ch 3, 2 dc in same sp, ch 2, * 3 dc in next ch-3 sp, ch 2; rep from * around, join to top of beg ch-3, fasten off.

- **Rnd 5:** Join Bright Dark Green with a Sl st in any ch-2 sp, ch 3, (1 dc, ch 2, 2 dc) in same sp. (Ch 2, shell in next ch-2 sp) around, ch 2, join to top of beg ch-3 with Sl st, fasten off. (16 ch-2 sps)

- **Rnd 6:** With I-9 hook, join Bright Light Green with a Sl st in any ch-2 sp of shell, ch 3, (2 dc, ch 3, 3 dc) in same sp. [Ch 1, 2 hdc in next ch-2 sp, ch 2, sc in next ch-2 sp of shell, ch 2, 2 hdc in next ch-2 sp, ch 1, (3 dc, ch 3, 3 dc) in next ch-2 sp of shell] around, ending ch 1, 2 hdc in next ch-2 sp, ch 2, sc in next ch-2 sp of shell, ch 2, 2 hdc in next ch-2 sp, ch 1, join to top of beg ch-3 with Sl st, fasten off.

- **Rnd 7:** Join White with Sl st in any corner ch-3 sp, 3 sc in same sp, * sc in each st and ch-sp across to next corner, 3 sc in corner sp; rep from * around, join with Sl st to beg sc. Fasten off and weave in all ends.

FLOWER BUDS (MAKE 63)
With H-8 hook and White yarn, ch 2, work 8 sc in second ch from hook, join to beg sc with Sl st. Fasten off and secure all ends.

JOINING
With RS facing and White yarn, whipstitch squares together with 10 rows of 8 squares each. See Fig. 1 for flower placement.

With white sewing thread, sew the flower buds over the square joining, as shown on Fig. 1.

Floral Bouquet

AFGHAN EDGING

- **Rnd 1:** With H-8 hook, join White yarn with a Sl st at seam before any corner, (sc, ch 3, dc) in same sp, * sk 2 sc (sc, ch 3, dc) in next sc/joining; rep from * across to within 1 sc of corner 3-sc group, [sk 1 sc, work (sc, ch 3, dc) in next sc] twice, sk 1 sc, (sc, ch 3, dc) in next sc; rep pat as established around entire afghan, join with Sl st to beg sc.

- **Rnd 2:** Sl st into ch-3 sp, (sc, ch 2, 2 dc) in same sp, [(sc, ch 2, 2 dc) in each ch-3 sp] around, join to beg sc. Fasten off and secure all ends.

PILLOW MATERIALS

- **4-ply worsted weight yarn**
  - -White (170 yds)
  - -Bright Dark Green (64 yds)
  - -Bright Light Green (64 yds)
  - -Light Pink (MC) (20 yds)
  - -Light Blue (MC) (20 yds)
  - -Light Coral (MC) (20 yds)
  - -Bright Yellow (MC) (20 yds)
  - -Dark Pink (CC) (1½ yds)
  - -Dark Blue (CC) (1½ yds)
  - -Medium Coral (CC) (1½ yds)
  - -Bright Gold (CC) (1½ yds)
- **Crochet hooks, size H-8 (5.0 mm), size I-9 (5.5 mm), and size J-10 (6 mm) or sizes to obtain gauge**
- **Tapestry needle**
- **Sewing needle**
- **White sewing thread**
- **14" pillow form**

PILLOW GAUGE One square = 6" × 6"

PILLOW DIRECTIONS

SQUARES (BACK)

Make one each with Light Coral, Bright Yellow, Light Blue, and Light Pink.

- **Rnd 1:** With H-8 hook and MC, ch 3, Sl st in third ch from hook to form a ring, ch 3, work 15 dc in ring, join with Sl st to top of ch-3. (16 dc)

- **Rnd 2:** Ch 3, 2 dc in same st as joining, ch 2, * sk next dc, 3 dc in next dc, ch 2; rep from * around, join with Sl st to top of beg ch-3, fasten off.

- **Rnd 3:** Join with Sl st in any ch-3 sp.

- **Rnds 4-6:** Rep Rnds 5-7 of afghan square.

Fig. 2 Pillow

Light Coral and Med. Coral	Bright Yellow and Bright Gold
Light Blue and Dark Blue	Light Pink and Dark Pink

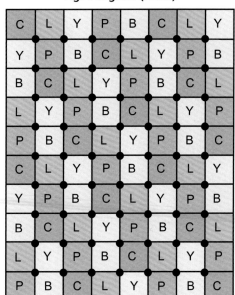

Fig. 1 Afghan (Front)

P	Light Pink (Rose)
B	Light Blue (Dark Blue)
L	Light Lavender (Lavender)
Y	Bright Yellow (Yellow)
C	Light Coral (Light Blue)
●	Flower Buds

SQUARES (FRONT)

Refer to afghan instructions and make 1 square of each color combination, except for Lavender, for a total of 4 squares.

FLOWER BUD (MAKE 1 FOR FRONT OF PILLOW)

Refer to afghan instructions.

JOINING

With RS facing, use White yarn to whipstitch flower squares (front) together, as shown on Fig. 2.

With RS facing, use White yarn to whipstitch squares (back) together, as shown on Fig. 2.

With white sewing thread, sew White bud over flower-square joining at dot shown on Fig. 2.

EDGING OF EACH FOUR-SQUARE PIECE

Starting at seam bet corners, use I-9 hook and White yarn to work edging of each four-square piece as instructed for afghan.

EDGING AND JOINING OF FRONT AND BACK

Place WS of front and back squares tog and join as follows: With J-10 hook and White yarn, start at any ch-3 sp of Rnd 2 of edging at joining, [(sc, ch 2, 2 dc) in both ch-3 sps] 6 times. (Sc, ch 2, 2 dc) in both scs, (sc, ch 2, 2 dc) in both ch-3 sps, (sc, ch 2, 2 dc) in both scs (this makes the corner). Cont with (sc, ch 2, 2 dc) in both ch-3 sps across to next corner, cont around entire pillow leaving an opening to insert pillow form. Cont with edging and joining. Join to beg sc, fasten off. ❖

Floral Bouquet II

Experimenting with colors allows you to create an afghan that fits your style. This alternate pattern for the Floral Bouquet afghan on the cover is equally stunning and is truly a delight to crochet.

DIRECTIONS

SQUARES

Make 16 squares of each contrasting color (CC) for a total of 80 squares.

Rnd 1: With H-8 hook and Dark Green, ch 2, work 8 sc in second ch from hook, join with Sl st to beg sc, fasten off.

Rnd 2: For petals, join CC with Sl st in any sc, ch 1, (sc, 2 dc) in same st and in each sc around, join with a Sl st to beg sc.

Rnd 3: Working behind petals of Rnd 1, Sl st bet first 2 sc, sc in same sp, ch 3, * sc bet next 2 sc, ch 3; rep from * around, join to beg sc. (8 ch-3 sps)

Rnd 4: Sl st in first ch-3 sp, ch 3, 2 dc in same sp, ch 2, * 3 dc in next ch-3 sp, ch 2; rep from * around, join to top of beg ch-3, fasten off.

Rnd 5: Join Dark Green with a Sl st in any ch-2 sp, ch 3, (dc, ch 2, 2 dc) in same sp, * ch 2, shell in next ch-2 sp; rep from * around, ch 2, join to top of beg ch-3, fasten off. (16 ch-2 sps)

Rnd 6: With I-9 hook, join Light Green with a Sl st in any ch-2 sp of shell, ch 3 (2 dc, ch 3, 3 dc) in same sp, * ch 1, 2 hdc in next ch-2 sp, ch 2, sc in next ch-2 sp of

AFGHAN II MATERIALS

- **4-ply worsted weight yarn**
  - Dark Green (10 oz, 520 yds)
  - Light Green (27 oz, 1,400 yds)
  - Rose (CC) (3 oz, 160 yds)
  - Blue (CC) (3 oz, 160 yds)
  - Light Blue (CC) (3 oz, 160 yds)
  - Lavender (CC) (3 oz, 160 yds)
  - Yellow (CC) (3 oz, 160 yds)
- **Crochet hooks, size H-8 (5.0 mm) and size I-9 (5.5 mm) or sizes to obtain gauge**
- **Tapestry needle**

shell; ch 2, 2 hdc in next ch-2 sp, ch 1, (3 dc, ch 3, 3 dc) in next ch-2 sp of shell; rep from * around, ending ch 1, 2 hdc in next ch-2 sp, ch-2, sc in next ch-2 sp of shell, ch 2, 2 hdc in next ch-2 sp, ch 1, join to top of beg ch-3 with Sl st.

Rnd 7: Sl st in next 2 dc and in corner ch-3 sp, ch 1, work 3 sc in same sp, * work 1 sc in each st and ch-sp across to next corner, work 3 sc in corner sp; rep from * around, join with Sl st to beg sc. Fasten off and weave in all ends.

FLOWER BUDS (MAKE 63)

With H-8 hook and Light Green ch 2, work 8 sc in second ch from hook, join with Sl st to beg sc. Fasten off and secure all ends.

JOINING

With RS facing and Light Green yarn, whipstitch squares together with 10 rows of 8 squares each. See Fig. 1 on page 18 for flower placement, referring to colors listed in parentheses.

With yarn ends, sew flower buds over square joining as shown on Fig. 1.

EDGING

Rnd 1: With H-8 hook, join Light Green yarn with a Sl st at seam before any corner, (sc, ch 3, dc) in same sp, * sk 2 sc (sc, ch 3, dc) in next sc/joining; rep from * across to within 1 sc of corner 3-sc group, [sk 1 sc, work (sc, ch 3, dc) in next sc] 3 times; rep pat as established around entire afghan, join with Sl st to beg sc.

Rnd 2: Sl st into ch-3 sp, (sc, ch 2, 2 dc) in same sp, (sc, ch 2, 2 dc) in each ch-3 sp around, join to beg sc. Fasten off and secure all ends. ❖

Double Wedding Ring
This lovely afghan makes the perfect wedding or anniversary gift and will be a treasured keepsake for a special couple. A crocheted interpretation of a time-honored quilt design, the afghan is worked in single, double, and treble crochet motifs and then joined.

Design by Maria Nagy of Sheffield Lake, Ohio

MATERIALS

- **4-ply worsted weight yarn**
  -White (55 oz)   -Multicolor (18 oz)
  -Lilac (15 oz)

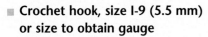

- **Crochet hook, size I-9 (5.5 mm) or size to obtain gauge**
- **Tapestry needle**
- **White sewing thread**   ■ **Sewing needle**

AFGHAN FINISHED SIZE
Approx 49" × 67"

AFGHAN GAUGE
First 2 rounds = 3¾" across center

STITCH GUIDE

tr (treble crochet): Yo twice, insert hook in designated st, yo and draw up a lp, (yo and draw through 2 lps) 3 times.

trcl (treble cluster): Keeping last lp of each st on hook, work 3 tr in designated st, yo and draw through all 4 lps on hook to form cluster.

DIRECTIONS

BASIC MOTIF (MAKE 35)
Note: All rows of Basic Motif are worked in the rnd.
With White, ch 6, join with Sl st to first ch to form ring.

- **Rnd 1:** (Sc in ring) 12 times, join with Sl st in first sc.

- **Rnd 2:** Ch 3 (counts as first tr), keeping last lp of each st on hook, work 2 more tr in same st, yo and draw through all 3 lps on hook (beg trcl made), (ch 3, trcl in next sc) 11 times, ch 3, join to top of beg trcl with a Sl st. (12 trcls and 12 ch-3 sps)

Note: Stop here and measure work; piece should measure 3¾" across center. If piece is larger than specified, ravel work and redo, using a smaller hook. If piece is smaller than specified, ravel work and redo using a larger hook. Measure piece routinely to ensure correct size. Measurement is listed after each rnd.

- **Rnd 3:** Ch 3, 3 dc in next ch-3 sp, (dc in top of next trcl, 3 dc in next ch-3 sp) 11 times, join to top of ch-3 with Sl st. (48 dc, 4⅞" across center)

- **Rnd 4:** Ch 3 (always counts as first dc), dc in same st, dc in each of next 3 dc, (2 dc in next dc, dc in each of next 3 dc) 11 times, join to top of ch-3 with Sl st. (60 dc, 6" across)

- **Rnd 5:** Ch 3, dc in same st. Working around in BLO, dc in each of next 4 dc, (2 dc in next dc, dc in each of next 4 dc) 11 times, join as before. (72 dc, 7⅛" across)

- **Rnd 6:** Ch 3, dc in same st. Working around in BLO, dc in each of next 5 dc, (2 dc in next dc, dc in each of next 5 dc) 11 times, join as before. (84 dc, 8¼" across)

- **Rnd 7:** Ch 3, dc in same st. Working around in BLO, dc in each of next 6 dc, (2 dc in next dc, dc in each of next 6 dc) 11 times, Sl st in top of ch-3, fasten off White. (96 dc, 9⅜" across)

MOTIF #4
(MAKE 1, USING 1 OF THE 35 BASIC MOTIFS)

- **Rnd 8:** With Sl st of Lilac on hook and working under both lps around, sc in any dc of Rnd 7 of Basic Motif, sc in each st around. Drop Lilac and insert hook into BLO of first sc of rnd, pull up a lp of Multicolor and pull through lp on hook, ch 1, fasten off Lilac. Do not turn. (96 sc, 9⅞" across)

CROCHETED-ON STRIP
Note: See Fig. 1.

- **Row 1:** With Multicolor and working across in BLO, sc in same st and in each of next 4 sc, (2 sc in next sc, sc in each of next 5 sc) twice. Ch 1, turn. (19 sc)

FIG. 1

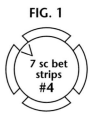

7 sc bet strips #4

- **Row 2:** Working across under both lps, 2 sc in first st, sc in each st across. Ch 1, turn. (20 sc)

- **Row 3:** Rep Row 2. Ch 1, fasten off Multicolor. Do not turn. (21 sc)

- **Row 4:** With Sl st on hook, join Lilac back in first sc of Row 1 with an sc on strip (where it meets motif). Working under both lps, sc in each row and each st around 3 sides of strip, having 2 sc in each outside corner. Fasten off Lilac. Sk next 7 Lilac sts on Rnd 8 of same Basic Motif. Insert hook in BLO of next st and draw up a lp of Multicolor, ch 1. Rep Rows 1-4 three more times. Weave all ends into like-colored sts. (17 sc for each strip, with 7 sc bet each strip in Rnd 8)

MOTIF #3
(MAKE 10, USING 10 OF
THE REM 34 BASIC MOTIFS)
Note: See Fig. 2.

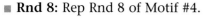

FIG. 2

- **Rnd 8:** Rep Rnd 8 of Motif #4.

- **Rows 1-4:** Rep Rows 1-4 of Crocheted-on Strip of Motif #4 three times.

MOTIF #2
(MAKE 24 FROM
REM 24 BASIC MOTIFS)
Note: See Fig. 3.

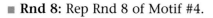

FIG. 3

- **Rnd 8:** Rep Rnd 8 of Motif #4.

- **Rows 1-4:** Rep Rows 1-4 of Crocheted-on Strip of Motif #4 twice.

Use a tapestry needle to tie a 6" piece of scrap yarn onto Rnd 8 of all the Motifs #3 at the 2 specified points (Fig. 2): 7 sts from each strip with 15 sts bet ties. Work same for all Motifs #2 (Fig. 3), with 7 sts bet the 2 middle ties. These ties will be used to tie the next motifs in place horizontally, then vertically. Do not remove ties until instructed to do so.

ASSEMBLY
Work this portion from right to left and from top to bottom. Referring to Fig. 4, place the second Motif #2 on top of the first Motif #2. * Bring up both ties from the lower motif through the upper motif at the points where the Crocheted-on Strip meets the Basic Motif. Tie the upper motif in place securely. *Note: Dashed lines represent the Rnd-8 edge of the lower motif.*

With a needle and sewing thread doubled, use a running stitch to sew the upper side of the first motif to the underside of the second motif along the edge of the Crocheted-on Strip (of the second motif) and Rnd 8 (of the first motif) as follows: Sew the motifs tog

picking up top of lps on lower motif and underside of lps on upper motif so no sts show through on either front or back of afghan (invisible sts). Tie off end of thread securely. Weave in ends. **

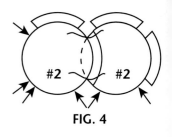

FIG. 4

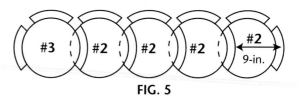

FIG. 5

One at a time, join next two Motifs #2 in the same manner. Join a Motif #3 on top of the fourth motif in the same manner, referring to Fig. 5. This completes Row 1. Set aside.

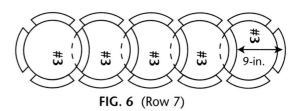

FIG. 6 (Row 7)

Make up Rows 2-6 separately in the same manner according to Fig. 5. Make up Row 7 by rotating four Motifs #3 one-quarter turn clockwise. Place Motif #4 at the end of the row (Fig. 6).

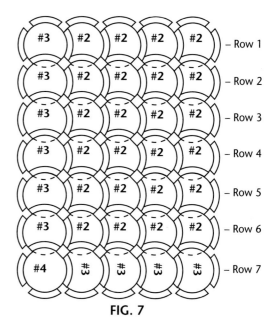

FIG. 7

JOINING
Working from bottom to top, place Row 7 on top of Row 6 and rep from * to ** in "Assembly." Cont joining

each row in turn, ending with Row 2 on top of Row 1 and referring to Fig. 7.

SEWN-ON STRIP (MAKE 82)
With Multicolor, ch 18.

- **Row 1:** Sc in second ch from hook and in each of next 4 chs, (2 sc in next ch, sc in each of next 5 chs) twice. Ch 1, turn. (19 sc)

- **Row 2:** 2 sc in first sc, sc in each st across. Ch 1, turn. (20 sc)

- **Row 3:** 2 sc in first sc, sc in each st across changing to Lilac in last step of last sc. Ch 1, fasten off Multicolor. Do not turn. (21 sc)

FIG. 8

- **Row 4:** With Lilac, and working under both lps, 2 sc in same st, sc around all 4 sides of strip having 2 sc in each corner, fasten off (RS). Weave in ends. *Note: Notice the side where beg ch was. This side is shorter than the other long side (see Fig. 8). Stop here and compare this strip to Crocheted-on Strips. If piece is different than Crocheted-on Strips, ravel work and redo using a larger or smaller hook. After 2 Sewn-on Strips have been crocheted, tie them RS up on the first Motif #2 in Row 1 exactly opposite their counterparts (making additional ties as needed). (See shaded areas on Fig. 9.) Each Sewn-on Strip must correspond to the overlapped portion of the "lower" Basic Motif, with corners of the "beg ch" side just touching the corners of the Crocheted-on Strips. Make 2 more Sewn-on Strips and tie them to the second Motif #2 in Row 1.*

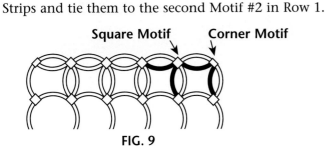

Square Motif **Corner Motif**

FIG. 9

SQUARE MOTIF (MAKE 44)
Note: See Fig. 9.

With 2 strands of White and a Sl st on the hook, ch 8.

- **Row 1:** Sc in second ch from hook and in each ch across. Ch 1, turn. (7 sc)

- **Rows 2-7:** Sc in each sc across, ch 1, turn, fasten off after Row 7. (Measures 2¾" × 2¾")

Stop here and tie first square motif to afghan in Row 1 bet first and second motifs, nestling it bet the 6 strips as shown in Fig. 9. If square is other than it should be, ravel work and redo using a smaller or larger hook.

CORNER MOTIF (MAKE 4)
Note: See Fig. 9.

Using 2 strands of White and having a Sl st on hook, ch 8.

- **Rows 1-3:** Rep Rows 1-3 of Square Motif, fasten off after Row 3. (Measures 2¾" × 1½")

Stop here and tie first corner motif to afghan in Row 1 at upper right corner, nestling it bet the 4 strips as shown in Fig. 9. If motif is different than it should be, ravel work and redo using a smaller or larger hook. Sew Sewn-on Motifs in place with invisible sts. Sew square and corner motifs in place with invisible sts in sides of sts and rows.

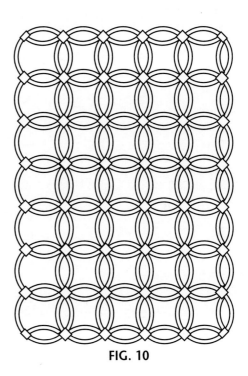

FIG. 10

Make the required amount of each of the 3 types of motifs. Cont across Row 1 sewing motifs in place with invisible sts, referring to Fig. 10. Work across each row systematically having all rows of square motifs going in the same direction. Each Motif #2 has 2 Sewn-on Strip motifs, each Motif #3 has 3 Sewn-on Strip motifs, and Motif #4 has 4 Sewn-on Strip motifs.

After all motifs have been joined, carefully remove all ties. With Sl st on hook, join Lilac with a Sl st in Lilac st next to White edge of any square motif, along perimeter. Sc across the 2 White sides of motif (having 2 sc in corner) and join with Sl st in next Lilac st. Fasten off. Weave in ends. Rep around entire outside edge of afghan, working across 2 sides of square motifs and 1 side of corner motifs. ❖

Eve's Coverlet

Worked in squares, joined, and then admired, this pretty afghan is as eye-catching as a blooming garden on a sunny spring morning! Long single crochets, decreases, and a popcorn variation give the afghan its textured, lacy look.

Design by Susan Stevens, East Lake, Ohio

AFGHAN FINISHED SIZE
Approx 53" × 73"

AFGHAN GAUGE
One square = 10" × 10"

MATERIALS

- **4-ply worsted weight yarn**
  -White (60 oz, 3,300 yds)
  -Sage (12 oz, 660 yds)
  -Off-white (6 oz, 330 yds)
  -Multicolor (15 oz, 780 yds)
- **Crochet hook,
  size G-6 (4.0 mm)
  or size to obtain gauge**
- **Tapestry needle**

STITCH GUIDE

FPsc (front post single crochet): Insert hook from front to back to front around the body or post of the sc. (Fig. 1)

Lsc (long single crochet): Work over the row just completed. Insert hook into st indicated and work sc as directed, pulling up the lp to fit over the previous row.

sc dec: Insert hook into first st, yo and draw through a lp in the first sc, insert hook into second st, yo, and draw through a lp; yo and draw through all 3 lps on hook.

3 tr pc: Work 3 tr into stitch specified; remove hook from stitch, insert it into both lps of the first tr worked, catch lp of last tr worked and pull through.

hdc (half double crochet): Yo and insert hook where indicated, catch yarn and draw a lp through the ch (3 lps on hook), yo and draw a lp through all 3 lps to complete st.

faux pc: Insert hook from front to back in sp to right of 4-dc group and back to front in sp on left of same 4-dc group. Yo, draw yarn through both sps, yo, draw yarn through 2 lps.

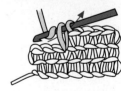

FIG. 1

DIRECTIONS

Note: Count carefully as you crochet, especially at ends of rnds, and at final joining of last rnd to square, to be sure your counts are accurate. This will enable you to join your squares stitch for stitch.

SQUARES (MAKE 25)
With Off-white, ch 4, join with Sl st to first ch.

- **Rnd 1:** Sc, work 9 dc in ring, do not join, end off. (Center bud made)

- **Rnd 2:** *Note: Work all sts behind Rnd 1. Work in sp between dc and down into foundation ring.*

With Off-white, join to Rnd 1 with Sl st, ch 4 between first and second dc of Rnd 1. (Sk 2 dc, sc into Rnd 1, ch 3) 3 times. Join with Sl st to second ch of ch-4. (4 ch-3 sps made)

- **Rnd 3:** (Sc, 6 dc, sc) in each ch-3 sp around. Do not join. (4 petals made)

- **Rnd 4:** Work behind Rnd 3, between dc, and down into Rnd-2 ch-3 sp. Sk next sc and dc. (Sc, ch 4, sk next 4 sts) 8 times. Join with Sl st to first sc. Fasten off Off-white.

■ **Rnd 5:** With Sl st of Sage, join in any ch-4 sp, 5 sc in same sp. (FPsc around next sc, 5 sc in next ch-4 sp) 7 times. FPsc around last sc. Join with Sl st to first sc.

■ **Rnd 6:** Sl st in next 2 sc. [Ch 2, (dc, ch 1, dc) in next FPsc, ch 2. Sk next 2 sc, Sl st in next sc] 8 times. Sl st in first Sl st to join, fasten off.

■ **Rnd 7:** *Note: Rnd 7 and similar rnds will "ruffle;" the next rnd will correct this.* With Multicolor, join with Sl st in any ch-1 sp, ch 2 (counts as first dc), 3 dc, ch 4, (4 dc, ch 4 over the top of next Sl st and down into the same Rnd-5 sc the Sl st used, 4 dc, ch 4 in next ch-1 sp) around, ending 4 dc in next Sl st, ch 4, join with Sl st to first dc. Fasten off. (16 4-dc groups made)

■ **Rnd 8:** With White, join with Sl st in ch-4 sp to the right of any 4-dc group. Work faux pc around same 4-dc group. (Dc, ch 4, dc over top of next ch-4 down into ch-2 sp of Rnd 6. Work faux pc around next ch-4 group) around, ending dc, ch 4, dc over top of next ch-4 group into ch-2 sp of Rnd 6, join with Sl st to first faux pc. (16 faux pcs made)

■ **Rnd 9:** (3 hdc, ch 1, 3 hdc in next ch-4 sp, FPsc around next sc dec) around. Join with Sl st to first hdc. (16 shells made)

■ **Rnd 10:** *Note: Rnd 10 and similar rnds will pull slightly; the next rnd will correct this.* Sl st in next 2 hdc, (Sl st in ch-1 sp, ch 4) around, join with Sl st to first Sl st. (16 ch-4 sps made)

■ **Rnd 11:** Sl st over top of first Sl st of Rnd 10 and down into ch-1 sp of shell on Rnd 9. (Sc, 7 hdc, sc in next ch-4 sp, Sl st down into ch-1 sp of shell) around, omitting last Sl st. Join with Sl st to first Sl st, fasten off. (16 scallops made)

■ **Rnd 12:** *Note: This rnd changes the circle into a square. It is important to place the corners properly, with the center roses pointing the same way. Hold the circle with center-bud overlap pointing down. The petals will point north, east, south, and west. Draw an imaginary line from the center bud to the east. The Rnd-11 scallop the line crosses is the beg place for Rnd 12. In this round, all sts are worked in the center (fifth) st of each scallop.* With Sl st on hook and White, join in this st, in the designated starting scallop. Ch 4, Sl st in next scallop, ch 4, * (3 tr pc, ch 7, 3 tr pc) in next scallop, (ch 4, Sl st in next scallop) 3 times, ch 4; rep from * twice, ending (3 tr pc, ch 7, 3 tr pc) in next scallop, ch 4, Sl st in next scallop, ch 4. Join to first Sl st with Sl st. (4 ch-7 corners and 16 ch-4 sps made)

■ **Rnd 13:** (6 sc in each ch-4 sp, 12 sc in each ch-7 corner sp) around. Join with Sl st to second sc at beg of rnd. (16 6-sc groups, 4 12-sc corners made)

■ **Rnd 14:** Ch 1, sc in next 4 sc. (Sk first sc, sc in next 5 sc of each 6-sc group across to corner. Sk beg sc of 12-sc group. Sc in next 5 sc, 3 sc in next sc, sc in next 5 sc) around. Join with Sl st in beg sc, end off White.

Rnd 15: *Note: Corner Lsc are worked into same sc on Rnd 13 the corner 3 sc used; all Lsc along sides are worked into skipped sc of Rnd 13.* With Sage and Sl st on hook, * (Lsc, ch 3) 4 times in corner sc of Rnd 13. (Lsc, ch 3) twice in each skipped sc of Rnd 13 across to corner; rep from * around. Join with Sl st to beg Lsc. Fasten off. (56 ch-3 sps made)

Rnd 16: With Multicolor and Sl st on hook, ch 3 in second ch of any corner ch-3. (4 dc, ch 3 in next ch-3 sp. Sl st, ch 3 in second ch of next ch-3) around, ending 4 dc, ch 3, join with Sl st to first Sl st, fasten off. (28 4-dc groups made)

Rnd 17: With White and Sl st on hook, join in ch-3 sp to right of any 4-dc group on east side of square. (Sc dec around next 4-dc group, dc, ch 3, dc over top of next Sl st and down into same ch the Sl st used) across to corner. (2 tr, ch 4, 2 tr over top of corner Sl st and down into ch-3 sp of Rnd 15) around, ending dc, ch 3, dc over top of next Sl st, join with Sl st to first sc dec.

Rnd 18: [3 hdc, ch 1, 3 hdc in next ch-3 sp. FPsc around next sc dec, across to corner. Hdc in next 2 tr. (Hdc, ch 1, 3 hdc, ch 1, hdc) in corner ch-4, hdc in next 2 tr, FPsc around next sc dec] around. Join with Sl st to first hdc. (24 shells, 4 corners made)

Rnd 19: Sl st in next 2 hdc. (Loosely work Sl st, ch 4 in each ch-1 sp of each shell across. Sl st, ch 7 in first ch-1 sp of corner. Sk center 3 hdc of corner. Sl st, ch 4 in second ch-1 sp of corner) around. Join with Sl st in third Sl st of beg.

Rnd 20: Rep Rnd 13. (28 6-sc groups, 4 12-sc corners made)

Rnd 21: Rep Rnd 14. End off. (28 5-sc groups, 4 13-sc corners made). At this point, recheck your gauge. Your square should measure 10". If it does not, switch to a larger or smaller hook.

JOINING

To start, lay down 2 squares, one above the other with RS up and center-bud overlap pointing south. Flip upper square down on top lower square, RS together. With White and working in BLO of both squares, (Sl st, ch 1) in each pair of sc across

TIP

When you make an afghan out of squares or any other shape, make a couple extras and stitch them to the back of the afghan. If you ever need to replace a square, simply use one of the extras. The color will match because it has been laundered with the rest of the blanket (and the dye lot will be the same).

to opposite corner. Do not cut yarn. Line up 2 more squares and join in the same way until 10 squares are joined (2 rows of 5 squares). End off. Check the ch-1 sps bet each pair of squares across to be sure they are not twisted. Add next row of 5 squares in this manner until you have 5 strips total. Join in the opposite direction with the same method.

BORDER

Rnd 1: All side Lsc are worked down into skipped sc of Rnd 20 and into each corner sc the corner 3 sc used on each side of square joining rows. Corner Lsc are worked into same sc the corner 3 sc used. With Sage and Sl st on hook, * (Lsc, ch 3) 4 times in corner sc. (Lsc, ch 3) twice in each designated st across side to corner; rep from * around. Join with Sl st to first Lsc.

Rnd 2: With Multicolor, rep Rnd 16 of square, end off.

Rnd 3: With White, rep Rnd 17 of square.

Rnd 4: Rep Rnd 18 of square.

Rnd 5: Sl st in next 2 hdc. Working loosely, (Sl st, ch 4 in each ch-1 sp) around. Join with Sl st in third Sl st in beg.

Rnd 6: Sl st over top of first Sl st of Rnd 3 and down into ch-1 sp of shell on Rnd 4. (Sc, 7 hdc, sc in next ch-4 sp. Sl st down into ch-1 sp of next shell on Rnd 4) around. Omit last Sl st and join with Sl st in first Sl st. Fasten off, secure all ends. ❖

Harlequin

This great take-along project uses a unique joining process that reduces the number of loose ends to weave in. It is as fun to crochet as it is to admire!

Design by Julie Chesbrough of Bellingham, Washington

AFGHAN FINISHED SIZE	AFGHAN GAUGE
Approx 52" × 72"	One square = 2" × 2"

STITCH GUIDE

hdc (half double crochet): Yo and insert hook where indicated, catch yarn and draw a lp through the ch (3 lps on hook), yo and draw a loop through all 3 lps to complete st.

bean stitch: (Yo, insert hook where indicated, yo and pull up a lp) twice, yo and pull through all 5 lps on hook, ch 1.

MATERIALS

- **4-ply worsted weight yarn**
  -Navy (18 oz)   -Black (18 oz)
  -Assortment of 19 other colors (6 oz each)
- **Crochet hook, size F-5 (3.75 mm) or size to obtain gauge**
- **Tapestry needle**

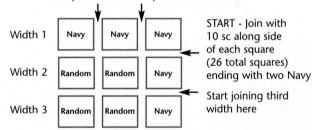

FIG. 1 These seams will be sewn lengthwise AFTER all squares have been joined widthwise.

START - Join with 10 sc along side of each square (26 total squares) ending with two Navy

Start joining third width here

DIRECTIONS

Note: Make 44 squares each of all colors except Navy and Black. Make 120 of Navy. Black is used for joining and edging only.

Ch 5, join with Sl st to first ch, do not turn.

- **Rnd 1:** Work 8 bean sts in ring, join with Sl st to first bean st, ch 1, do not turn.

- **Rnd 2:** Work 2 bean sts in first ch-1 sp, (work 1 bean st in next ch-1 sp, work 2 bean sts in next ch-1 sp) 3 times; work 1 bean st in last ch-1 sp, join with Sl st to first bean st, ch 1, do not turn.

- **Rnd 3:** Work 1 sc in same st, [3 sc, ch 1, 3 sc in next ch-1 sp (sp between 2-bean-stitch cluster), 2 sc in next 2 ch-1 sps] 3 times, 3 sc, ch 1, 3 sc in next ch-1 sp, 2 sc in next ch-1 sp, 1 sc in first ch-1 sp, join to first sc with Sl st. Fasten off and weave in ends.

JOINING

Note: You will be joining your afghan squares together first entirely widthwise, then entirely lengthwise, not in individual strips of squares as you may be accustomed to doing. This method eliminates many loose ends that would need to be woven in. Take two squares of Navy and hold WS together. With Black yarn and Sl st on hook, * insert hook in back lps of corner sc, skipping the corner ch-1 sp, sc in back lps of each stitch; rep across side, working 10 total sc. Do not end off. Using next a border color and a random color from the mixed squares; rep from * (Fig. 1).

Continue in this manner, working with Navy and random color squares, until you have 25 total attached. Use 2 squares of Navy for the 26th join. You have now made 2 "widths" of your afghan. Go back to the starting end of the widths, and start a new width by joining a Navy square to the first Navy square, a random square to the next random square, repeating the process across as before, ending with a Navy square. Join 32 more widths of random colors with Navy on each end. The last width (#36) will be all in Navy.

Turn "one-way joined" afghan sideways. Starting at the edge, put the Navy unfinished length and the random unfinished length WS together. Join Black yarn in back lps of corner sc of both squares on the edge of afghan. * 10 sc in back lps of sc on both squares across, ch 1 across intersection; rep from * across the entire length, end off. Rep this process across all of the un-joined lengths.

EDGING

With Sl st on hook, join Black in any corner. Ch 2, 1 hdc, ch 1, 2 hdc in corner; hdc evenly spaced across side of afghan (10 hdc in each side, 1 hdc in each joining will give you an even edge), * (2 hdc, ch 1, 2 hdc) in corner, hdc evenly spaced across side of afghan; rep from * twice, join with Sl st to top of ch-2. End off and weave in all ends. ❖

Rosebud Afghan
Instructions begin on page 32.

Keepsake Afghans
FOR BABY

Hand-knit or crocheted blankets are one of the best ways to express your joy upon the arrival of a new baby. Whether you stitch one for your own little one or give it as a gift to an expectant couple, the afghans presented in the following pages will quickly become treasured keepsakes.

There's nothing more comforting than snuggling with a soft, subtly colored afghan like the "Rosebud" design, and nothing brightens up a nursery more than the vibrant "Baby Brights" blanket. The "Roses in the Snow" afghan adds a delightful touch to a baby's room, and "Twinkle, Little Star" and "Sail Away" are perfect for a special little girl's or boy's themed room.

Knit or crochet more than one of these lovely designs, and keep them on hand for when you need a one-of-kind gift. Experiment with different colors, so each new baby in your life can have a unique afghan to cherish for a lifetime.

Rosebud

A sweet gift for for a little one, this darling blanket is knit with soft green and pink yarn and embellished with pink ribbon. It will quickly become a favorite snuggly for a girl or a boy.

Design by Barbara Todd, Imperial, Missouri

MATERIALS

- **4-ply worsted weight yarn**
  -Soft Green (14 oz, 738 yds)
  -White (7 oz, 369 yds)
  -Soft Pink (3 oz, 158 yds)

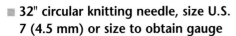

- **32" circular knitting needle, size U.S. 7 (4.5 mm) or size to obtain gauge**
- **14" single-point knitting needles, size U.S. 7 (4.5 mm) or size to obtain gauge**
- **Tapestry needle**
- **6 yds ³⁄₈"-wide pink ribbon**

AFGHAN FINISHED SIZE
Approx 33" × 38"

AFGHAN GAUGE
18 sts and 32 rows = 4"

SPECIAL ABBREVIATIONS
(k1, p1) in yo-twice: Knit into first lp of the yo-twice, sl this lp off left needle; purl into second lp of yo-twice, sl this lp off left needle.

WYB: With yarn in back

WYF: With yarn in front

DIRECTIONS

With circular needle and White, cast on 125 sts.

- **Row 1 (WS):** Purl across.
- **Rows 2-3:** With Soft Green, knit across.

Note: When instructed to sl a stitch, sl as if to purl.

- **Row 4:** With White, k2, * WYB sl 1, k7; rep from * across to last 3 sts, WYB sl 1, k2.
- **Row 5:** With White, p2, * WYF sl 1, p7; rep from * across to last 3 sts, WYF sl 1, p2.
- **Row 6:** With Soft Green, k2, * WYB sl 1, k7; rep from * across to last 3 sts, WYB sl 1, k2.
- **Row 7:** With Soft Green, k2, * WYF sl 1, k7; rep from * across to last 3 sts, WYF sl 1, k2.
- **Row 8:** With White, k6, * WYB sl 1, k7; rep from * across to last 7 sts, WYB sl 1, k6.
- **Row 9:** With White, p6, * WYF sl 1, p7; rep from * across to last 7 sts, WYF sl 1, p6.
- **Row 10:** With Soft Green, k6, * WYB sl 1, k7; rep from * across to last 7 sts, WYB sl 1, k6.
- **Row 11:** With Soft Green, k6, * WYF sl 1, k7; rep from * to last 7 sts, WYF sl 1, k6.

Rep Rows 4-11 for pat. Cont in pat rep until afghan measures approx 32" from cast-on edge. End with Row 11.

- **Last 2 Rows:** With White, knit 1 row across, purl 1 row across. Bind off all sts in knit.

BORDER
With straight needles and Soft Green, cast on 15 sts.

Note: When instructed to sl a stitch, sl as if to knit. Yo sts tend to twist around the needle. Be sure you are working into the correct lp of the yos.

- **Row 1:** Sl 1, k1, yo, k2tog, k3, yo, k2tog, k1, yo, p2tog, k1, yo twice, k2.
- **Row 2:** K2, (k1, p1) in yo-twice, k1, yo, p2tog, yo, k2tog, k8.
- **Row 3:** Sl 1, k1, yo, k2tog, k3, yo, k2tog, k1, yo, p2tog, k5.
- **Row 4:** BO first 2 sts, k2, yo, p2tog, yo, k2tog, k8.

Rep Rows 1-4 until border is long enough to fit around body of afghan allowing for ease at corners and ending by working Row 4. BO.

FIG. 1

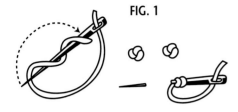

EMBROIDERY

With tapestry needle and Soft Pink yarn, use photo and chart below as a placement guide and add French knots. Weave Soft Pink yarn into sts on WS when going from one French knot to the next. For French knots, wrap yarn around needle twice. (Fig. 1)

FINISHING

With tapestry needle and Soft Green, sew straight edge of border to body of afghan, easing to fit at corners. Sew first row to last row of border. Weave in all loose ends.

Cut two pieces of ribbon 50" each in length and two pieces 58" each in length. Weave one 50" piece of ribbon through the eyelets in the top border, and one in the bottom border. Weave one 58" piece of ribbon through the eyelets in each side of the border. Tie in a bow at each corner. ❖

TIP

To increase or decrease the finished size of your project, count the number of stitches in the repeat of the pattern. Next, see the gauge to determine how many stitches you will need to add to achieve the size you want. Add the number of repeats that come closest to the number of inches you wish to add (or subtract).

For example, with the Rosebud afghan, if you wish to make this 4" wider (the finished width is 33" and you would like to make your afghan 37" wide) look first to the gauge. This says that 18 sts = 4". Next look to the pattern repeat. The pattern repeat begins in Row 4. The repeat is 8 stitches. Two repeats would be 16 stitches. Adding 16 stitches would give you nearly 37" in width. You would need to cast on 141 stitches.

Remember to also increase (or decrease) the yarn quantities required. Adding 4" to the width increases the size by approximately 10 percent (33 divided by 37 = .89). Increase your yarn quantities accordingly.

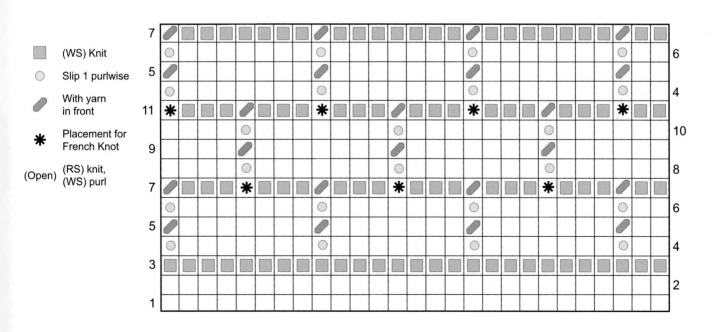

(WS) Knit

Slip 1 purlwise

With yarn in front

Placement for French Knot

(Open) (RS) knit, (WS) purl

Twinkle, Little Star

Your little one will have sweet dreams with this heavenly afghan in his or her nursery. A fantastic gift for a girl or a boy, it is a great take-along project as you work each diamond and triangle separately and then join them together.

Design by Cheryl Helbig of New Milford, New Jersey

AFGHAN FINISHED SIZE
Approx 41" × 57"

AFGHAN GAUGE
With J-10 hook and worsted weight yarn: 14 dsc = 4"
With G-6 hook and sport weight yarn: 20 sc = 4"

STITCH GUIDE

sc dec: Insert hook into first st, yo and draw through 1 lp on hook, insert hook into next st, yo, and draw through 1 lp on hook, yo and draw through all 3 lps on hook.

To attach yarn with sc: Place lp of slipknot on hook. Insert hook into designated st, draw up lp. Yo, draw through 2 lps on hook.

dsc (double single crochet): Insert hook into next st, yo and pull up lp, yo and draw through 1 lp on hook, yo and draw through 2 lps on hook.

dsc dec (double single crochet decrease): Insert hook into first st, yo and pull up lp, yo and draw through 1 lp on hook, insert hook into next st, yo and pull up lp, yo and draw through 1 lp on hook, yo and draw through 3 lps on hook.

MATERIALS

- **4-ply worsted weight yarn**
  -White (21 oz, 1,141 yds)
  -Blue (12 oz, 652 yds)
  -Yellow (12 oz, 652 yds)

- **3-ply sport weight yarn**
  -Light Blue (6 oz, 471 yds)
  -Light Yellow (6 oz, 471 yds)

- **Crochet hooks, size G-6 (4.0 mm) and size J-10 (6.0 mm) or sizes to obtain gauge**

- **Tapestry needle**

- **6 yds each ³⁄₈"-wide sheer ribbon in Light Blue and Light Yellow**

- **Stitch marker**

- **Straight pins**

DIRECTIONS

DIAMONDS
(MAKE 6 EACH OF BLUE, YELLOW, AND WHITE)

- **Row 1:** Using J-10 hook and worsted weight yarn, ch 2, 2 dsc in second ch from hook. Ch 1, turn. (2 dsc)

- **Row 2:** 2 dsc in each of next 2 sts. Ch 1, turn. (4 dsc)

- **Row 3:** 2 dsc in first st, dsc in each st across to last st, 2 dsc in last st. Ch 1, turn. (6 dsc)

- **Rows 4-18:** Rep Row 3. Ch 1, turn. (36 dsc in Row 18)

- **Row 19:** Work even in dsc. Ch 1, turn.

- **Row 20:** Dsc dec in first 2 sts, dsc in each st across to last 2 sts, dsc dec. Ch 1, turn. (34 dsc)

- **Rows 21-37:** Rep Row 20. Ch 1, Do not turn at end of last row. (1 dsc in Row 37)

- **Edging:** Sc evenly around outer edge of Diamond, working 3 sc in each top, bottom, and side point. Fasten off.

CORNER TRIANGLE (MAKE 4 WHITE)

- **Row 1:** Using J-10 hook and White, ch 2, 2 dsc in second ch from hook. Ch 1, turn. (2 dsc)

- **Row 2:** Dsc in first st, 2 dsc in next st. Ch 1, turn. (3 dsc)

- **Row 3:** 2 dsc in first st, dsc in each rem st. Ch 1, turn. (4 dsc)

- **Row 4:** Dsc in each st to last st, 2 dsc in last st. Ch 1, turn. (5 dsc)

- **Rows 5-18:** Rep Rows 3 and 4. Ch 1, turn. (19 dsc in Row 18)

- **Row 19:** Work even in dsc. Ch 1, do not turn.
- **Edging:** Sc evenly around outer edge of Triangle, working 3 sc in each of 3 points. Fasten off.

TOP/BOTTOM TRIANGLE (MAKE 4 WHITE)

- **Rows 1-19:** Using J-10 hook and White, work same as Diamond. Ch 1, Do not turn at end of Row 19.
- **Edging:** Sc evenly around outer edge of Triangle, working 3 sc in each of 3 points. Fasten off.

SIDE TRIANGLES (MAKE 6 WHITE)

- **Rows 1-18:** Work same as Corner Triangle.
- **Row 19:** Work even in dsc. Ch 1, turn. (19 dsc)
- **Row 20:** Dsc in each st to last 2 sts, dsc dec. Ch 1, turn.
- **Row 21:** Dsc dec in first 2 sts, dsc in rem sts. Ch 1, turn.
- **Rows 22-37:** Rep Rows 20 and 21. Ch 1, do not turn at the end of Row 37.
- **Edging:** Sc evenly around outer edge of Triangle, working 3 sc in each of 3 points. Fasten off.

MOON (MAKE 6 LIGHT YELLOW)

- **Row 1:** Using G-6 hook and Light Yellow sport weight yarn, ch 12, sc in second ch from hook and in each ch across. Ch 1, turn. (11 sc)
- **Row 2:** 2 sc in first st, sc in each st across, 2 sc in last st. Ch 1, turn. (13 sc)
- **Rows 3-8:** Rep Row 2. (25 sc in Row 8)
- **Row 9:** Sc in first 10 sts, leave rem sts un-worked, turn, do not ch 1. (10 sc)
- **Row 10:** Sl st in first st, 9 sc across short row. Ch 1, turn. (9 sc)
- **Row 11:** Sc in next 8 sts, Sl st in last st. Turn, do not ch 1. (8 sc)
- **Rows 12-18:** Rep Rows 10 and 11, but each row's sc total will dec by one. (1 sc in Row 18) Fasten off.
- **Row 19:** Sk next 5 un-worked sts on Row 8. Attach yarn with sc in next st, sc in next 9 sts. Ch 1, turn. (10 sc)
- **Row 20:** Sc in first 9 sts, Sl st in last st, turn, do not ch 1. (9 sc)
- **Row 21:** Sl st in first sc, sc across. Ch 1, turn. (8 sc)
- **Rows 22-28:** Rep Rows 20 and 21, but each row's sc total will dec by one. Ch 1, do not turn. (1 sc in Row 28)

- **Edging:** Sc in each st and at end of each row around with 3 sc in each of 2 points. Join with Sl st. Fasten off leaving 30" tail for sewing Moon to Diamond.

STAR (MAKE 6 LIGHT BLUE)

- **Rnd 1:** Using G-6 hook and Light Blue sport weight yarn, ch 2, 5 sc in second ch from hook. Do not join. Place stitch marker at beg of each rnd. (5 sc)
- **Rnd 2:** 2 sc in each sc around. (10 sc)
- **Rnd 3:** (Sc in next sc, 2 sc in next sc) rep around. (15 sc)
- **Rnd 4:** (Sc in next 2 sc, 2 sc in next sc) rep around. (20 sc)
- **Rnd 5:** (Sc in next 3 sc, 2 sc in next sc) rep around. (25 sc)
- **Rnd 6:** (Sc in next 4 sc, 2 sc in next sc) rep around. (30 sc)
- **Rnd 7:** Work even in sc, Sl st in first sc of rnd to join. Ch 1, do not turn. (30 sc) Now work in rows.

FIRST POINT

- **Row 1:** Sc in next 6 sc. Ch 1, turn. (6 sc)
- **Rows 2-3:** 6 sc, ch 1, turn. (6 sc)
- **Row 4:** Sc dec, sc in next 2 sc, sc dec. Ch 1, turn. (4 sts)
- **Rows 5-6:** 4 sc, ch 1, turn. (4 sc)
- **Row 7:** (Sc dec) twice. Ch 1, turn. (2 sts)
- **Rows 8-9:** 2 sc, ch 1, turn. (2 sc)
- **Row 10:** Sc dec. (1 st) Fasten off.

SECOND POINT

- **Row 1:** Attach yarn with sc in next un-worked st on Rnd 7, sc in next 5 sc. Ch 1, turn. (6 sc)
- **Rows 2-10:** Rep Rows 2–10 of First Point.

THIRD, FOURTH, AND FIFTH POINTS

Rep Rows 1-10 of Second Point three more times. At end of last row of Fifth Point, ch 1, turn.

EDGING

Work 3 sc in last sc of Row 10. Sc in end of each row along sides of each point, Sl st bet sts in Rnd 7. Cont to sc around edge of Star working 3 sc in tip of each point and Sl st bet sts in Rnd 7. Join with Sl st to first sc in edging. Fasten off leaving 30" tail for sewing.

Placement Diagram

■ Blue Ribbon
● Yellow Ribbon

ASSEMBLY

Note: Refer to color photo on page 34 and placement diagram above.

1. Pin a Moon to center of each Blue Diamond. Use a tapestry needle and 30" tail to sew in place.

2. Pin a Star to center of each Yellow Diamond. Use a tapestry needle and 30" tail to sew in place.

3. Sew Diamonds tog alternating Moon and Star Diamonds and placing White Diamonds bet each row. Sew Side Triangles into place. Sew Top and Bottom Triangles into place. Sew Corner Triangles into place.

BORDER

■ **Row 1:** With J-10 hook, join White with sc in any corner, sc evenly around edge, working 3 sc in each corner. Join with Sl st in first sc. Ch 1, turn.

■ **Row 2:** Sc in each sc around, working 3 sc in center sc of each corner. Join with Sl st in first sc. Fasten off.

■ **Row 3:** Turn, join Yellow worsted weight yarn with sc in same st as joining, sc in each sc around, working 3 sc in center sc of each corner. Ch 1, turn.

■ **Rows 4-6:** Rep Row 2. At end of Row 6, fasten off.

■ **Row 7:** With Blue worsted weight yarn, rep Row 3.

■ **Rows 8-12:** Rep Row 2. At end of Row 12, fasten off. With tapestry needle, weave ends into WS of work.

BOW PLACEMENT

Following the placement diagram, apply ribbon to points of the Diamonds. Using tapestry needle, bring ribbon ends from back to front at each Diamond point. Tie a bow on RS of afghan. ❖

Baby Brights
Add a splash of color to your favorite tot's nursery with this quick-to-crochet keepsake afghan. The vibrantly colored throw will stand out among the pastel hues found in many babies' rooms.

Design by Monica Costello of Hannibal, Ohio

MATERIALS

- **4-ply worsted weight yarn**
  -White (A) (12½ oz, 700 yds)   -Green (D) (6 oz, 350 yds)
  -Pink (B) (6 oz, 350 yds)   -Blue (E) (6 oz, 350 yds)
  -Yellow (C) (6 oz, 355 yds)
- **Crochet hook, size J-10 (6.0 mm) or size to obtain gauge**
- **Tapestry needle**
- **Stitch holder**

AFGHAN FINISHED SIZE
Approx 38" × 40"

AFGHAN GAUGE
12 sc and 16 rows = 4"

STITCH GUIDE
pc (popcorn): Yo hook, insert hook into sc and draw up lp, (yo hook, insert hook into same sc, and draw up lp) 3 times, yo hook and draw through all 9 lps on hook. Ch 1 to secure the pc. The pc will show on the reverse side, which is the RS. When working with the RS facing, sc through the large lp (the ch) of each pc in the previous row.

PATTERN NOTES
- This baby afghan is worked in panels. When completing a panel, use a stitch holder to temporarily hold the last st securely, until it is to be joined to the next panel. Do not cut the yarn.
- Panels are joined as they are completed. Take care when joining panels to place them in the same direction and follow the panel number sequence shown on the placement chart (on page 40).
- When ready for panel joining, with RS facing, pick up dropped lp (on stitch holder) of right panel. Hold this panel and next (left) panel tog, WS facing. Insert hook into the row ends of each panel (through the right and then left panel). Pull yarn through both thicknesses and lp on hook, working a Sl st. Cont joining panels tog with Sl st, matching the row ends very carefully. At the lower end of the panel, work the last Sl st through the end ch of the foundation ch of each panel.
- For less yarn ends to weave into fabric, join each panel after it is completed, cont to use the working yarn for joining the panels.
- When weaving ends into work after the panels have been joined, weave toward and then into the joined seams. This will keep yarn ends neatly hidden in the seams.

DIRECTIONS

PANEL #1
(FIRST PANEL ON RIGHT SIDE OF AFGHAN)
- **Row 1 (RS):** With color B, ch 11, sc into second ch from hook and in each ch across. Ch 1, turn. (10 sc)
- **Row 2 (WS):** 4 sc, pc, sc, pc, 3 sc. Ch 1, turn. (10 sc)
- **Row 3:** Sc across. Ch 1, turn. (10 sc)
- **Row 4:** 3 sc, pc, 3 sc, pc, 2 sc. Ch 1, turn. (10 sts)
- **Row 5:** Rep Row 3. (10 sc)
- **Rows 6-163:** Rep Rows 2–5 until 40 pc groups have been completed, ending with a Row 3 (which is a RS row). Do not fasten off or cut yarn. Place last lp on hook onto a stitch holder.

PANEL #2
- **Row 1 (RS):** With color A, ch 8, sc into second ch from hook and in each ch across. Ch 1, turn. (7 sc)
- **Row 2 (WS):** 3 sc, pc, 3 sc. Ch 1, turn. (7 sc)
- **Rows 3-5:** Sc across. Ch 1, turn. (7 sc)

PANEL PLACEMENT CHART

The number in each column refers to the panel-number pattern to be worked. The letter refers to the yarn color.

Start Joining ↓

4-E	2-A	3-D	2-A	3-C	2-A	3-B	2-A	3-E	2-A	3-D	2-A	3-C	2-A	1-B

- **Rows 6-163:** Rep Rows 2–5 until 41 pc have been completed, ending with a Row 3 (which is a RS row). Do not fasten off or cut yarn. Place last lp on hook onto a stitch holder.

PANEL #3
(MAKE 2 EACH FROM COLORS C AND D; MAKE 1 EACH FROM COLORS B AND E)

- **Row 1 (RS):** Ch 12, sc in second ch from hook and in each ch across. Ch 1, turn. (11 sc)

- **Row 2 (WS):** 4 sc, pc, sc, pc, 4 sc. Ch 1, turn. (11 sts)

- **Row 3:** Sc across. Ch 1, turn. (11 sc)

- **Row 4:** 3 sc, pc, 3 sc, pc, 3 sc. Ch 1, turn. (11 sts)

- **Row 5:** Rep Row 3.

- **Rows 6-163:** Rep Rows 2–5 until 40 pc groups have been completed, ending with a Row 3 (which is a RS row). Do not fasten off or cut yarn. Place last lp on hook onto a stitch holder.

PANEL #4
(LAST PANEL ON LEFT SIDE OF AFGHAN)

- **Row 1 (RS):** With color E, ch 11, sc in second ch from hook and in each ch across. Ch 1, turn. (10 sc)

- **Row 2 (WS):** 3 sc, pc, sc, pc, 4 sc. Ch 1, turn. (10 sts)

- **Row 3:** Sc across. Ch 1, turn. (10 sc)

- **Row 4:** 2 sc, pc, 3 sc, pc, 3 sc. Ch 1, turn. (10 sts)

- **Row 5:** Rep Row 3.

- **Rows 6-163:** Rep Rows 2–5 until 40 pc groups have been completed, ending with a Row 3 (which is a RS row). Do not fasten off or cut yarn. Place last lp on hook onto a stitch holder.

JOINING

Following the placement chart above and pattern notes on page 38, work afghan from right to left, joining panels as instructed. At the end of Panel 4-E, ch 1. Fasten off.

EDGING

Note: Work after all panels are joined.

- **Rnd 1:** With RS facing and color A, pull up lp in the top right corner sc. Ch 1, 2 sc in same corner, 8 sc across Panel 1-B. * At the joining seam, insert the hook through the loose lp of yarn at the end of the panel. With the lp on the hook, sk the first sc of the next panel. ** *Note: Picking up the loose lps at the seams will result in a neater edging at the panel joinings on this rnd.*

Sc into center 5 sc of Panel 2-A; rep from * to **. Sc into center 9 sc of Panel 3-C; rep from * to **. Cont working across the top edge of the afghan in the same manner, repeating from * to ** at the panel seam joinings. 3 sc in the last sc at top left corner sc.

Working on the side edge, sk 1 row, (sc into edge of the next 3 rows, sk 1 row) to next corner, ending the last rep with sk 1 row, 3 sc into the next corner sp on the foundation ch edge.

Work into free lps of foundation ch in same manner as for top edge (pulling up the lp at the panel seams and same stitch counts). Work 3 sc into the next corner sp.

Work the other side edge same as first side edge. End the rnd with sc into the base of the beg 2 sc at the top right corner. Join with Sl st to beg sc. (464 sc) Ch 1, turn.

- **Rnd 2 (WS):** 2 sc into first sc at top right corner. Sc into each sc around, working 3 sc into center sc of each corner. End the rnd with sc into same sp as beg 2 sc. Join with Sl st to first sc. (472 sc) Ch 4, turn. (Ch 4 counts as dc plus ch-1 on next rnd)

- **Rnd 3 (RS):** Dc into base of ch-4, sk 1 sc, * (dc in next sc, ch 1, sk 1 sc) rep to corner sc. ** In the corner sc, (dc, ch 1) 3 times, sk 1 sc. Rep from * twice, then rep from * to ** once. In same st as beg ch (dc, ch 1), Sl st into third ch of beg ch-4. Ch 1, turn.

- **Rnd 4 (WS):** 2 sc into same st as Sl st, sc into each ch-1 sp and each dc around afghan, working 3 sc into each corner dc. End the rnd with sc into base of beg 2 sc. Join with Sl st to first sc of the rnd. Ch 3, turn.

- **Rnd 5 (RS):** (Sl st into the third ch from the hook, Sl st into the sc above the dc in Rnd 3, ch 3) around the entire afghan edge. Sl st into base of beg ch-3, fasten off. Weave ends into WS of afghan. ❖

TIP

Make a sample swatch before beginning your project not only to check your gauge, but also to determine if you like the texture and thickness of the stitch pattern. For a thicker stitch, try holding two strands of yarn together and crocheting with the recommended hook. For a softer, thick stitch, use two strands of yarn and crochet with a larger hook. Remember, changing how many strands you use and adjusting hooks sizes will affect your gauge and the finished size of the afghan; therefore, you will need to purchase additional yarn.

Roses in the Snow

This delicate design is a stunning example of how beautiful crochet can be. Think how proud parents would be to bring their baby home from the hospital wrapped in this afghan, or show off the new arrival to friends and family!

Design by Michelle Crean of Benton Harbor, Michigan

AFGHAN FINISHED SIZE
Approx 39" × 48"

AFGHAN GAUGE
One block = 4¾" × 4¾"
20 sts and 12 rows = 4" in basketweave pattern

STITCH GUIDE

shell: 7 dc in st specified in pattern.

V-st: (Dc, ch 1, dc) in st specified in pattern.

FPdc (front post double crochet): Yo, insert hook from front around the post of next st, coming out again at the front or other side of post, yo, draw up a lp, (yo, draw though 2 lps) twice. (Fig. 1)

BPdc (back post double crochet): Yo, insert hook from back around the post of next st, coming out again at the back or other side of post, yo, draw up a lp, (yo, draw though 2 lps) twice. (Fig. 2)

Note: When working either FPdc or BPdc, always sk the st behind the post.

MATTERIALS

- **3-ply baby weight yarn**
  -White (22¾ oz, 2,288 yds)
- **Crochet hooks, size D-3 (3.25 mm) and size F-5 (3.75 mm) or size to obtain gauge**
- **Tapestry needle**
- **8 yds ⅜"-wide white ribbon**

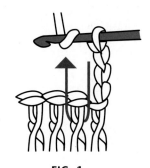

FIG. 1

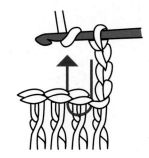

FIG. 2

DIRECTIONS

ROSE BLOCKS (MAKE 28)

Note: Turn your block only when indicated.

With D-3 hook, ch 3. Join with Sl st to first ch to form ring.

- **Rnd 1:** (Sc in ring, ch 3) 8 times, join with Sl st to first sc.
- **Rnd 2:** Ch 1, (sc, ch 1, hdc, ch 1, sc) in each ch-3 around. (8 petals) Join with Sl st to first sc. Ch 1, turn.
- **Rnd 3:** Working around the posts of sc in Rnd 1, sc around first sc, ch 3, (sc around next sc, ch 3) 7 times, join with Sl st to first sc. Ch 1, turn.
- **Rnd 4:** (Sc, ch 1, hdc, ch 1, hdc, ch 1, sc) in each ch-3 sp around, join with Sl st to first sc. Ch 1, turn.
- **Rnd 5:** Rep Rnd 3, working in posts of sc in Rnd 3.
- **Rnd 6:** [Sc, ch 1, (hdc, ch 1) 3 times, sc] in each ch-3 sp around, join with Sl st to first sc.
- **Rnd 7:** Working in BLO for this rnd, Sl st to center hdc. Ch 1, (3 dc, ch 2, 3 dc) in same st, ch 3, sc in center hdc of next petal, ch 3, * (3 dc, ch 2, 3 dc) in center hdc of next petal, ch 3, sc in center hdc of next petal, ch 3; rep from * around. Join with Sl st to top of first dec.

- **Rnd 8:** Ch 1, (dc, ch 1, dc) in same st as joining, [sk next 2 dc, (V-st, ch 2, V-st) in corner ch-2 sp, sk next 2 dc, V-st in next dc, sk ch-3, V-st in sc, sk ch-3 sp, V-st in next dc] 3 times; (V-st, ch 2, V-st) in corner, sk next 2 dc, V-st in next dc, sk ch-3, V-st in next sc, sk next ch-3, join with Sl st to top of first dc.

- **Rnd 9:** Ch 1, sc in first dc, sc in each ch-1 sp and dc to corner ch-2 sp, [(sc, ch 2, sc) in corner, sc in each dc and ch-1 sp across to corner] 3 times, (sc, ch 2, sc) in corner, sc in each rem dc and ch-1 sp across. Join with Sl st to first sc. (15 sc along each side, not including corners)

- **Rnd 10:** Ch 1, dc in first sc, dc in each rem sc to corner ch-2 sp, [(dc, ch 2, dc) in corner, dc in each sc across to corner] 3 times, (dc, ch 2, dc) in corner, dc in each rem sc across. Join with Sl st to top of first dc. (17 dc along each side, not including corners)

- **Rnd 11:** Ch 1, sc in joining and each dc to corner sp [(sc, ch 2, sc) in corner sp, sc in each dc to corner] 3 times, (sc, ch 2, sc) in corner sp, sc in each rem dc. Join with Sl st to first sc. (19 sc along each side, not including corners) End off yarn, fasten and secure ends.

JOINING BLOCKS

Using a tapestry needle and White yarn, hold blocks tog with RS facing and match st for st. Sew through both lps of sc starting with second ch-1 sp in first corner across to first ch-1 sp of next corner. Make 4 strips of 7 blocks each. Sew end blocks of each strip tog so you have a 7-block-by-9-block rectangle. Set aside.

INSIDE BORDER

Working around inside of blocks, join yarn in last sc of any side. With D-3 hook, ch 1, sc in last sc, [(sc last un-worked ch-1 of this square, sp between joinings on corner block, and first un-worked ch-1 of next square tog) for corner, sc in each sc and ch-1 sp of blocks to corner] around. Join with Sl st to first sc, end off. (113 sc across top and bottom, 159 sc across each side, not counting 4 corner sc)

BASKETWEAVE CENTER

With size F-5 hook and White yarn, ch 108.

- **Row 1:** Dc in second ch from hook and in each ch across. Ch 1, turn. (107 dc)

- **Row 2:** Hdc in first dc, BPdc around next 3 dc, (FPdc around next 3 dc, BPdc around next 3 dc) across, hdc in last dc. Ch 1, turn.

- **Row 3:** Hdc in hdc, FPdc around next 3 dc, (BPdc around next 3 dc, FPdc around next 3 dc) across, hdc in last hdc. Ch 1, turn.

- **Row 4:** Hdc in hdc, FPdc around next 3 dc, (BPdc around next 3 dc, FPdc around next 3 dc) across, hdc in last hdc. Ch 1, turn.

- **Row 5:** Hdc in hdc, BPdc around next 3 dc, (FPdc around next 3 dc, BPdc around next 3 dc) across, hdc in last hdc. Ch 1, turn.

- **Row 6:** Hdc in hdc, FPdc around next 3 dc, (BPdc around next 3 dc, FPdc around next 3 dc) across, hdc in last hdc. Ch 1, turn.

- **Row 7:** Hdc in hdc, FPdc around next 3 dc, (BPdc around next 3 dc, FPdc around next 3 dc) across, hdc in last hdc. Ch 1, turn.

- **Row 8:** Hdc in hdc, BPdc around next 3 dc, (FPdc around next 3 dc, BPdc around next 3 dc) across, hdc in last hdc. Ch 1, turn.

- **Row 9:** Hdc in hdc, FPdc around next 3 dc, (BPdc around next 3 dc, FPdc around next 3 dc) across, hdc in last hdc. Ch 1, turn.

- **Rows 10-99:** Rep Rows 4-9 fifteen times.

- **Rows 100-102:** Repeat rows 4-6. After Row 102, change to size D-3 hook. You will now start working in rnds.

- **Rnd 1:** With D-3 hook, 2 sc in first hdc (mark first sc as corner); sc in top of next 105 dc, 2 sc in next hdc (mark second sc as corner); working in sides of rows, (2 sc in next hdc, sc in next hdc) down side; working in opposite side of starting ch, 2 sc in first ch (mark first sc as corner st), sc in next 105 sts, 2 sc in last st (mark second sc as corner); working up sides of rows, 2 sc in next hdc, sc in next hdc) up side. Join with Sl st to first sc. (107 sc × 153 sc)

- **Rnd 2:** Ch 1, [3 sc in corner sc (mark center sc as corner), sc in each sc to corner] around. Join with Sl st to first sc.

- **Rnd 3:** Ch 1, (dc, ch 1, dc, ch 1, dc) in corner sc, ch 1, sk next sc, (dc in next sc, ch 1, sk next sc) to corner, [(dc, ch 1, dc, ch 1, dc) in corner sc, sk next sc, (dc in next sc, ch 1, sk next sc) to corner] around. Join with Sl st to top of first dc.

Rnd 4: Ch 1, sc in each dc and ch-sp around, marking sc over center dc of each shell as corner dc for matching blanket center to rose border later. Join with Sl st to first sc, end off, fasten and secure ends.

Matching corner to corner and sc for sc, sew blanket center to inside of rose block rectangle, using White yarn and tapestry needle.

OUTSIDE BORDER

Rnd 1: With D-3 hook, join yarn in corner sp before long edge. Ch 1, [3 sc in corner sp, sc in each sc across block, sc in ch-1 sp before joining, sk joining, (sc in un-worked ch-1 at beg of block, sc in each sc across block, sc in un-worked ch at end of block, sk joining) across to last block, sc in un-worked ch at beg of block, sc in each sc across block] around. Join with Sl st to first sc. (161 sc × 207 sc, not counting corner sc)

Rnd 2: Ch 1, sc in first sc, (3 sc in corner, sc in each sc to corner) around. Join with Sl st to first sc.

Rnd 3: Ch 1, dc in first sc, ch 1, sk next sc, [(dc, ch 1, dc, ch 1, dc) in corner sc, ch 1, sk next sc, (dc in next sc, ch 1, sk next sc) across to corner] around. Join with Sl st to top of first dc.

Rnd 4: Ch 1, sc in each dc and ch-1 sp around, join with Sl st to first sc. *Note: Mark sc over center dc of corner for corner.*

Rnd 5: Ch 1, sc in first 4 sc, (3 sc in corner sc, sc in each rem sc to corner) around. Join with Sl st to first sc. (169 sc across top and bottom and 215 sc along each side, not counting 4 corner sc groups)

Rnd 6: Ch 1, shell in next sc, sk next sc, sc in next sc, sk next sc, shell in corner. Long Edge: Sk next 2 sc, (sc in next sc, sk next sc, shell in next sc, sk next 2 sc) across, shell in corner sc. First Short Edge: Sk 1 sc, sc in next sc, sk next sc, shell in next sc, (sk next 2 sc, sc in next sc, sk next 2 sc, shell in next sc) to last 3 sc before corner, sk next sc, sc in next sc, sk next sc, shell in corner sp. Rep Long Edge. Second Short Edge: Sk 1 sc, sc in next sc, sk next sc, (shell in next sc, sk next 2 sc, sc in next sc, sk next 2 sc) across, sk last sc. Join with Sl st to top of first dc of first shell.

Rnd 7: Ch 1, [sc in first dc of shell, (ch 1, sc in next dc) 6 times, sk next sc] around. Join with Sl st to first sc.

Rnd 8: Ch 1, [sc in ch-1 sp, (ch 2, sc in next ch-1 sp) 5 times, sk next 2 sc] around. Join with Sl st to first sc.

Rnd 9: Ch 1, [sc in ch-2 sp, (ch 2, sc in next ch-2 sp) 4 times, sk next 2 sc] around. Join with Sl st to first sc.

Rnd 10: Ch 1, [sc in ch-2 sp, (ch 3, sc in next ch-2 sp) 3 times, sk next 2 sc] around. Join with Sl st to first sc.

Rnd 11: Ch 1, [sc in ch-3 sp, ch 4, (sc, ch 3, sc in previous sc) in next ch-3 sp (picot made), ch 4, sc in next ch-3 sp, sk next 2 sc] around. Join with Sl st to first sc. End off, fasten and secure all ends.

FINISHING

Thread ribbon through Rnd 3 of blanket center; trim ends and tack tog with sewing needle and white thread on WS of work. Tack corners square.

Thread 4½ yds of ribbon through Rnd 3 of outside border; trim ends and tack tog on WS of work. Tack corners square. ❖

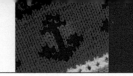
Sail Away

The special child in your life will adore snuggling with this imaginative knit creation as he or she drifts off to dreamland. Duplicate stitches add detail to the nautical design.

Design by Georgia Vincent of Pittsfield, New Hampshire

AFGHAN FINISHED SIZE
Approx 34" × 41"

AFGHAN GAUGE
16 sts and 22 rows = 4"

STITCH GUIDE

duplicate stitch: Bring yarn to the outside at the base of the st below the st to be duplicated. Pull yarn through to front. Place needle from right to left behind both sides of the st above the one being duplicated. Complete the st by returning the needle to where you began. When working a series of horizontal duplicate stitches, complete one st and begin the adjacent st in one step. (See Fig. 1)

St st (stockinette stitch): Knit every RS row; purl every WS row.

skpo: With yarn in back, sl 1, k1, psso. (1 st dec)

FIG. 1

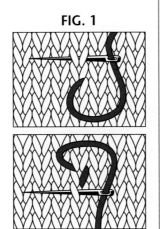

MATERIALS

- **4-ply worsted weight yarn**
  - Dark Blue (7 oz, 380 yds)
  - Light Blue (3.5 oz, 190 yds)
  - Red (3.5 oz, 190 yds)
  - Blue (3.5 oz, 190 yds)
  - White (3.5 oz, 190 yds)
  - Yellow (3.5 oz, 190 yds)
  - Black (3.5 oz, 190 yds)
  - Light Brown (3.5 oz, 190 yds)
  - Green (3.5 oz, 190 yds)
  - Teal (3.5 oz, 190 yds)
  - Optional (if you do not wish to change colors for fish): Multicolor (3 oz, 167 yds)
- **14" single-point knitting needles, size U.S. 7 (4.5 mm) or size to obtain gauge**
- **Crochet hook, size H-8 (5.0 mm) or size to obtain gauge**
- **Tapestry needle**

WHAT IS DUPLICATE STITCH?

Duplicate stitch models the knit stitch, but it is actually embroidery worked on the surface of the knitted fabric. It is often used to add color details like in the larger sailboat picture or for small motifs like the small sailboat motif in the border. You can also use it to correct small mistakes.

DIRECTIONS

Note: The large sailboat, except for smaller accent areas, is to be knit in as you go. When picking up new colors in the body of your work, be sure to pick the yarn up from underneath to avoid holes in your work. Smaller accent areas are to be worked in duplicate stitch at your discretion.

CENTER

With Dark Blue, cast on 67 sts and work in St st. Follow the chart, for 30 rows.

Change to Light Blue for the background and work 102 rows, following the chart. (132 rows total) BO.

Work the smaller areas in duplicate stitch, following the color chart. Embroider an inverted "V" using Black

backstitches for the roof of the lighthouse. Work the top stitch on the mast loosely.

Optional: Personalize by embroidering a name on the bow of the boat.

TOP/BOTTOM BORDER

With White and RS facing, pick up 67 sts evenly spaced, along bottom. Turn. WS: Knit across.

- **Row 1:** (K2tog, yo) across to last st, k1.
- **Row 2:** Knit across, drop White.
- **Row 3:** With Blue and White alternating, (k1 Blue, k1 White) across, ending with k1 Blue. Drop White.

Sail Away

- **Row 4:** With Blue, purl across.

- **Rows 5-20:** Starting 3 sts in from ends and keeping 4 sts bet each motif, work anchor chart 5 times. (67 sts)

- **Row 21:** Knit across.

- **Row 22:** Pick up Dark Blue and (p1 Dark Blue, p1 Blue) across, ending p1 Dark Blue. Drop Blue.

- **Rows 23-24:** With Dark Blue, knit across.

- **Row 25:** Rep Row 1.

- **Rows 26-27:** Knit across.

- **Row 28:** (K1, p1) across, ending k1.

- **Row 29:** Knit across.

- **Rows 30-33:** Rep Rows 28 and 29 twice. BO on WS. Rep this border on the top edge.

BORDER SIDES

With White and RS facing, pick up 95 sts, turn. WS: Knit across.

- **Rows 1-4:** Rep Rows 1-4 of Top/Bottom Border.

- **Row 5-22:** Starting 4 sts in from ends and keeping 4 sts bet each motif, work anchor chart 7 times. (95 sts)

- **Rows 23-35:** Rep Row 23-35 of Top/Bottom Border.

CORNERS (MAKE 4)

Note: Duplicate stitch sailboat motif when corners are finished.

With Dark Blue, cast on 35 sts, turn.

- **Row 1 (WS):** (K1, p1) across, ending k1.

- **Row 2:** Skpo, knit across to last 2 sts, k2tog. (33 sts)

- **Row 3:** (P1, k1) across, ending p1.

- **Row 4:** Rep Row 2. (31 sts)

- **Row 5:** (K1, p1) across, ending k1.

- **Row 6:** Rep Row 2. (29 sts)

- **Row 7:** Knit across.

- **Row 8:** Skpo, (k2tog, yo) across to last 3 sts, k1, k1 and sl back to left needle. Pass last st over knitted st and sl to right needle. (27 sts)

- **Rows 9-10:** Rep Row 2. (23 sts)

- **Row 11:** Purl across. (23 sts)

  Work in St st, dec 1 st each side on every knit row until 5 sts rem, ending on last dec (knit) row.

  WS: P2tog, p1, p1 and sl back to left needle. Pass last st over and sl back to right needle.

  RS: Sl 1, k2tog, psso. End off.

FINISHING

Duplicate stitch sailboat on each corner by starting on the third row of St st, centering design and following the small sailboat chart. Join corners by laying corner pieces over the sides and using H-8 crochet hook with your yarn in back of the afghan, Sl st through both pieces toward the center. End off. Rep for rem corners.

With tapestry needle and Red yarn, work a running st along the side of the sailboat as indicated by red line on chart.

EDGING

With H-8 crochet hook, join Dark Blue with Sl st in any corner of the afghan. * Sc in next st, hdc in next st, (dc, ch 3, Sl st in first ch, dc) in next st, hdc in next st, sc in next st; rep from * around, Sl st to first sc to join. End off, fasten and secure all ends. ❖

Sailboat Border

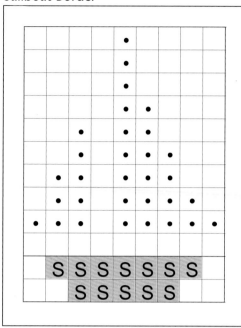

Sailboat Border Motif Key (duplicate stitch

| • | White | S | Red |

Small Anchor Border

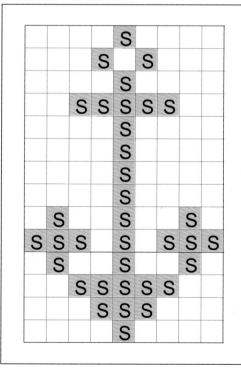

Small Anchor Border Motif Key

| S | Red |

Large Sailboat

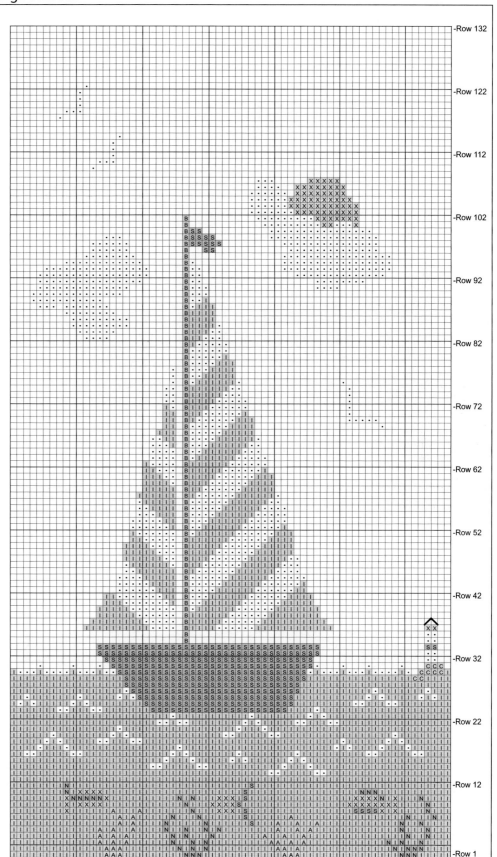

Sail Away Key

COLOR

•	White
X	Yellow
C	Black
I	Dark Blue
S	Red
N	Green
A	Teal
B	Light Brown
	Light Blue

BACKSTITCH

— Black

RUNNING STITCH

— Red

Shoots and Ladders Afghan
Instructions begin on page 52.

Knit Afghans
FOR ANY HOME

Whether you're a knitter who desires a challenge or you just want sit back, relax, and enjoy your favorite pastime, you'll find just what you are looking for in this collection of award-winning knit afghans. From rich colors to pretty pastels, there is something to suit any setting. And these afghans aren't just beautiful—they'll keep you warm on blustery days, too!

You'll enjoy working every stitch as you create the wonderful textures in "Shoots and Ladders" and "Summer Woods," which are as cozy and comforting as they appear. The delicate cables and pastel hues of "Lilac Fantasy" add softness to any setting, and the color options for "Sonoma" make it easy to adapt to your personal style.

After you've knit the last stitch, reward yourself by curling up with your favorite book and your newest handmade afghan— and enjoy the compliments you are sure to receive!

Shoots and Ladders

Discover delightful detail in this impressive knit afghan. Worked in panels with stunning colors and textures, you'll delight in the variety of stitching as you increase and decrease to create the three-dimensional design.

Design by Susan Kerin of Ocean Pines, Maryland

MATERIALS

- **4-ply worsted weight yarn**
  - -Green (35 oz, 1,820 yds)
  - -Red (5 oz, 230 yds)
  - -Gold (4 oz, 200 yds)
  - -Tan (4 oz, 200 yds)
  - -Gray (8 oz, 420 yds)
  - -Black (4 oz, 200 yds)
- **Knitting needles, size U.S. 6 (4.0 mm) or size to obtain gauge**
- **Crochet hook, size G-6 (4.0 mm)**
- **Tapestry needle**

AFGHAN FINISHED SIZE
Approx 55" × 55"

AFGHAN GAUGE
16 sts = 4" on a plain
St st swatch

STITCH GUIDE

inc as to p (increase as to purl): Purl into front and then into back of next st.

inc as to k (increase as to knit): Knit into front and then into back of next st.

garter stitch: Knit across.

skpo: With yarn in back, sl 1, k1, psso. (1 dec)

DIRECTIONS

SEED STITCH PANEL (MAKE 3)

With Green, cast on 50 sts.

Work garter stitch for 20 rows. Then work in pat as follows:

- **Row 1:** K6, * k2, p2; rep from * across row to last 6 sts, k6.
- **Row 2:** K6, * p2, k2; rep from * across row to last 6 sts, k6.
- **Row 3:** Rep Row 2.
- **Row 4:** Rep Row 1.

Rep Rows 1-4 for a total of 320 rows. Work garter stitch for 20 rows. BO. (360 rows)

SHOOTS PANEL (MAKE 2)
FIRST PANEL

With Green, cast on 49 sts. Work garter stitch for 20 rows. Then work in pat as follows:

- **Row 1 (RS):** K10, p13, k3, p13, k10.
- **Row 2:** K5, p5, k13, p3, k13, p5, k5.
- **Row 3:** K10, p11, p2tog, inc as to k, k1, inc as to k, p2tog, p11, k10.

- **Row 4:** K5, p5, k12, p5, k12, p5, k5.
  Note: From this point on the number of sts in the pat varies from row to row, due to the 3-dimensional effect of the leaf pattern. As a guide, the number of sts is given at the end of each row in parentheses.
- **Row 5:** K10, p10, p2tog, yo, k1, yo, k3, yo, k1, yo, p2tog, p10, k10. (51 sts)
- **Row 6:** K5, p5, k11, p3, inc as to p, p1, inc as to p, p3, k11, p5, k5. (53 sts)
- **Row 7:** K10, p9, p2tog, k1, yo, k1, yo, k1, p2, k1, p2, k1, yo, k1, yo, k1, p2tog, p9, k10. (55 sts)
- **Row 8:** K5, p5, k10, p5, k1, inc as to k, p1, inc as to k, k1, p5, k10, p5, k5. (57 sts)
- **Row 9:** K10, p8, p2tog, k2, yo, k1, yo, k2, p3, k1, p3, k2, yo, k1, yo, k2, p2tog, p8, k10. (59 sts)
- **Row 10:** K5, p5, k9, p7, k1, inc as to k, k1, p1, k1, inc as to k, k1, p7, k9, p5, k5. (61 sts)
- **Row 11:** K10, p7, p2tog, k3, yo, k1, yo, k3, p3, k3, p3, k3, yo, k1, yo, k3, p2tog, p7, k10. (63 sts)
- **Row 12:** K5, p5, k8, p9, k1, inc as to k, k1, p3, k1, inc as to k, k1, p9, k8, p5, k5. (65 sts)
- **Row 13:** K10, p6, p2tog, k4, yo, k1, yo, k4, p4, k3, p4, k4, yo, k1, yo, k4, p2tog, p6, k10. (67 sts)

- **Row 14:** K5, p5, k7, p11, k1, inc as to k, k2, p3, k2, inc as to k, k1, p11, k7, p5, k5. (69 sts)
- **Row 15:** K10, p5, p2tog, skpo, k7, k2 tog, p5, k3, p5, skpo, k7, k2 tog, p2tog, p5, k10. (63 sts)
- **Row 16:** K5, p5, k6, p9, k5, inc as to p, p1, inc as to p, k5, p9, k6, p5, k5. (65 sts)
- **Row 17:** K10, p4, p2tog, skpo, k5, k2tog, p5, yo, k1, yo, p1, k1, p1, yo, k1, yo, p5, skpo, k5, k2tog, p2tog, p4, k10. (63 sts)
  Note: Be careful when purling the yarn overs in Row 17, as these tend to twist around the needle when going from knit to purl sts, and from purl to knit sts.
- **Row 18:** K5, p5, k5, p7, k5, p3, inc as to k, p1, inc as to k, p3, k5, p7, k5, p5, k5. (65 sts)
- **Row 19:** K10, p3, p2tog, skp, k3, k2tog, p5, k1, yo, k1, yo, k1, p2, k1, p2, k1, yo, k1, yo, k1, p5, skp, k3, k2tog, p2tog, p3, k10. (63 sts)
- **Row 20:** K5, p5, k4, p5, k5, p5, k1, inc as to k, p1, inc as to k, k1, p5, k5, p5, k4, p5, k5. (65 sts)
- **Row 21:** K10, p2, p2tog, skpo, k1, k2tog, p5, k2, yo, k1, yo, k2, p3, k1, p3, k2, yo, k1, yo, k2, p5, skpo, k1, k2tog, p2tog, p2, k10. (63 sts)
- **Row 22:** K5, p5, k3, p3, k5, p7, k1, inc as to k, p3, inc as to k, k1, p7, k5, p3, k3, p5, k5. (65 sts)
- **Row 23:** K10, p1, p2tog, k3tog, p5, k3, yo, k1, yo, k3, p3, k3, yo, k1, yo, k3, p5, k3 tog, p2tog, p1, k10. (63 sts)
- **Row 24:** Rep Row 12. (65 sts)
- **Row 25:** Rep Row 13. (67 sts)
- **Row 26:** Rep Row 14. (69 sts)
- **Row 27:** K10, p5, p2tog, skpo, k7, k2tog, p6, yo, k1, yo, p6, skpo, k7, k2tog, p2tog, p5, k10. (65 sts)
- **Row 28:** K5, p5, k6, p9, k6, p3, k6, p9, k6, p5, k5. (65 sts)
- **Row 29:** K10, p6, skpo, k5, k2tog, p6, k1, yo, k1, yo, k1, p6, skpo, k5, k2tog, p6, k10. (63 sts)
- **Row 30:** K5, p5, k6, p7, k6, p5, k6, p7, k6, p5, k5. (63 sts)
- **Row 31:** K10, p6, skpo, k3, k2tog, p6, k2, yo, k1, yo, k2, p6, skpo, k3, k2tog, p6, k10. (61 sts)
- **Row 32:** K5, p5, k6, p5, k6, p7, k6, p5, k6, p5, k5. (61 sts)
- **Row 33:** K10, p6, skpo, k1, k2tog, p6, k3, yo, k1, yo, k3, p6, skpo, k1, k2tog, p6, k10. (59 sts)
- **Row 34:** K5, p5, k6, p3, k6, p9, k6, p3, k6, p5, k5. (59 sts)
- **Row 35:** K10, p6, k3tog, p6, k4, yo, k1, yo, k4, p6, k3tog, p6, k10. (57 sts)
- **Row 36:** K5, p5, k13, p11, k13, p5, k5. (57 sts)
- **Row 37:** K10, p13, skpo, k7, k2tog, p13, k10. (55 sts)
- **Row 38:** K5, p5, k13, p9, k13, p5, k5. (55 sts)

- **Row 39:** K10, p13, skpo, k5, k2tog, p13, k10. (53 sts)
- **Row 40:** K5, p5, k13, p7, k13, p5, k5. (53 sts)
- **Row 41:** K10, p13, skpo, k3, k2tog, p13, k10. (51 sts)
- **Row 42:** K5, p5, k13, p5, k13, p5, k5. (51 sts)
- **Row 43:** K10, p13, skpo, k1, k2tog, p13, k10. (49 sts)
- **Row 44:** K5, p5, k13, p3, k13, p5, k5. (49 sts)
- **Row 45:** K10, p13, k3tog, p13, k10. (47 sts)
- **Row 46:** K5, p5, k12, inc as to k, k1, inc as to k, k12, p5, k5. (49 sts)
- **Row 47:** K10, p29, k10. (49 sts)
- **Row 48:** K5, p5, k29, p5, k5. (49 sts)

Work garter stitch for 10 rows.
Change to Gold. Work garter stitch for 10 rows.
Rep Rows 1-48 of panel pat. Work garter stitch for 10 rows.
Change to Gray. Work garter stitch for 10 rows.
Rep Rows 1-48 of panel pat. Work garter stitch for 10 rows.
Change to Tan. Work garter stitch for 10 rows.
Rep Rows 1-48 of panel pat. Work garter stitch for 10 rows.
Change to Red. Work garter stitch for 10 rows.
Rep Rows 1-48 of panel pat. Work garter stitch for 20 rows.
BO while knitting.

SECOND PANEL

With Red, cast on 49 sts. Work garter stitch for 20 rows. Follow as for first panel with color change next to Tan, then Gray, then Gold, then Green.

FINISHING

With Green and tapestry needle, join panels per photo. Attach Gray at top of afghan, pick up and knit 1 st in each st across. Knit 30 rows. BO in knitting. Attach Gray to bottom and rep as for top.

BORDER

- **Row 1:** Join Black in any corner with Sl st and crochet hook, work single crochet around outer edge, with 3 sc in each corner. Join to first sc with Sl st.
- **Row 2:** Sc through back lp of each sc around. Join with Sl st, fasten off.

OUTLINING COLOR BLOCKS

With RS up, hold Black yarn on WS of afghan. Beg at lower end of each section, insert crochet hook into first st bet 2 colors. Pull up a lp of Black. Insert hook into next st up, and pull up a lp of Black. Pull this lp through the first lp on hook. (Sl st made) Cont up the afghan bet each of the colors. Fasten off yarn. Weave in on WS. ❖

Sonoma

The soothing colors in this classy coverlet are reminiscent of the beautiful Sonoma Valley. A blend of knit and purl stitches creates a lacy look while the Grape stitch adds dimension to the beautiful blanket.

Design by Marguerite Wilson of New Brighton, Minnesota

AFGHAN FINISHED SIZE
Approx 41" × 62"

AFGHAN GAUGE
20 sts and 28 rows = 4" on a plain St st swatch using size 7 needles. Each square will measure approx 5½" × 5½" after working the sc rnd.

STITCH GUIDE
ssk: (Sl 1, sl 1) as if to knit, knit these 2 sts tog through back lp.

Grape: (K1, p1, k1, p1, k1) in st to make 5 sts from 1, turn, p5, turn, k5, turn, p5, turn; pass second, third, fourth, and fifth sts over first st, then knit in back of this st.

LCO (loop cast on): Make lp around left thumb, insert right needle in lp as to knit, sl lp off thumb onto right needle to make new st.

sk2po: Sl 1, k2tog, pass the slipped st over the k2tog st.

MATERIALS

- **3-ply worsted weight yarn**
  - Light purple (18 oz, 1,260 yds)
  - Dark purple (9 oz, 630 yds)
  - Off-white (12 oz, 840 yds)
- **Straight knitting needles, size U.S. 7 (4.5 mm) and size U.S. 6 (4.0 mm) or size to obtain gauge**
- **Crochet hook, size G-6 (4.0 mm)**
- **Tapestry needle**

DIRECTIONS

COLOR BLOCK A:
BUNCH OF GRAPES (MAKE 15)
With Dark Purple and size 6 needles, cast on 25 sts.

- **Rows 1 and 3 (RS):** Purl across.
- **Rows 2 and 4:** Knit across.
- **Row 5:** P12, Grape, p12.
- **Row 6:** Knit across.
- **Row 7:** Purl across.
- **Row 8:** Knit across.
- **Row 9:** P10, Grape, p3, Grape, p10.
- **Row 10:** Knit across.
- **Row 11:** Purl across.
- **Row 12:** Knit across.
- **Row 13:** P8, (Grape, p3) twice, Grape, p8.
- **Row 14:** Knit across.
- **Row 15:** Purl across.
- **Row 16:** Knit across.
- **Row 17:** P6, (Grape, p3) 3 times, Grape, p6.
- **Row 18:** Knit across.
- **Row 19:** Purl across.
- **Row 20:** Knit across.
- **Row 21:** Rep Row 13.
- **Row 22:** K10, p5, k10.
- **Row 23:** P9, k2tog, k1, yo, k1, yo, k1, ssk, p9.
- **Row 24:** K9, p7, k9.
- **Row 25:** P8, k2tog, k2, yo, k1, yo, k2, ssk, p8.
- **Row 26:** K8, p9, k8.
- **Row 27:** P7, k2tog, k3, yo, k1, yo, k3, ssk, p7.
- **Row 28:** K7, p11, k7.
- **Row 29:** P7, k1, k2tog, LCO, ssk, yo, k1, yo, k2tog, LCO, ssk, k1, p7.
- **Row 30:** K7, p2, k1, p5, k1, p2, k7.
- **Row 31:** P7, k2tog, LCO, p1, LCO, ssk, k1, k2tog, LCO, p1, LCO, ssk, p7.
- **Row 32:** K7, p1, k3, p3, k3, p1, k7.

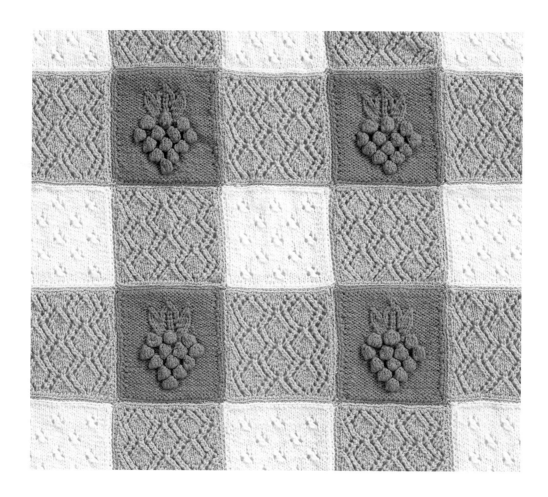

- **Row 33:** P11, LCO, sk2po, LCO, p11.
- **Row 34:** K12, p1, k12.
- **Row 35:** Purl across.
- **Row 36:** Knit across.
- **Row 37:** Purl across.

BO while knitting, do not fasten off. Drop lp from needle, insert crochet hook in lp. Ch 1, turn.
RS facing, work sc evenly around block, working 3 sc in each corner. Fasten off.

COLOR BLOCK B: LATTICE (MAKE 38)
With Light Purple and size 7 needles, cast on 25 sts.

- **Row 1 and all WS Rows:** Purl across.
- **Row 2:** K1, * k1 (k2tog, yo) twice, k1, (yo, ssk) twice, k2; rep from * once.
- **Row 4:** K1, * (k2tog, yo) twice, k3, (yo, ssk) twice, k1;, rep from * once.

- **Row 6:** K2tog, * yo, k2tog, yo, k5, yo, ssk, yo, sk2po; rep from * once, ending last rep with ssk instead of sk2po.
- **Row 8:** K1, * (yo, ssk) twice, k3, (k2tog, yo) twice, k1; rep from * once.
- **Row 10:** K1, * k1, (yo, ssk) twice, k1, (k2tog, yo) twice, k2; rep from * once.
- **Row 12:** K1, * k2, yo, ssk, yo, sk2po, yo, k2tog, yo, k3; rep from * once.

Rep Rows 1-12 twice more.

BO while purling. Work sc around block as in Block A.

COLOR BLOCK C (MAKE 24)
With Off-white and size 7 needles, cast on 25 sts.

- **Rows 1, 3, and 5:** Purl across.
- **Rows 2 and 4:** Knit across.

TIP

Experimenting with different colors makes knitting even more enjoyable. To create the equally stunning version of the Sonoma afghan, at left, simply replace the Purple yarns with Aqua.

- **Row 6 (RS):** K3, yo, sk2po, yo, * k5, yo, sk2po, yo; rep from * once, end with k3.

- **Row 7:** Purl across.

- **Row 8:** K4, yo, ssk, * k6, yo, ssk; rep from * once. End with k3.

- **Row 9:** Purl across.

- **Row 10:** Knit across.

- **Row 11:** Purl across.

- **Row 12:** K2, * k5, yo, sk2po, yo; rep from * once, end with k7.

- **Row 13:** Purl across.

- **Row 14:** K8, * yo, ssk, k6; rep from * once, end with k1.

- **Rows 15-26:** Rep Rows 3-14.

- **Rows 27-35:** Rep Rows 3-11.

- **Row 36:** Knit across.

BO while purling. Work sc around block as in Block A.

FINISHING

Sew blocks tog in rows following placement chart.

EDGING

Work outer edging with White and G-6 hook.

- **Rnd 1:** Join with Sl st, ch 1, sc around afghan, working 3 sc in each corner. Sl st in first sc to join.

- **Rnd 2:** (Ch 3, sc in third ch from hook, sk next sc, sc in next sc) rep around. *Note: Do not sk sc in corners.* Sl st in first sc to join. Fasten off. ❖

Sonoma Placement Chart

	●		●		●	
●	□	●	□	●	□	●
	●		●		●	
●	□	●	□	●	□	●
	●		●		●	
●	□	●	□	●	□	●
	●		●		●	
●	□	●	□	●	□	●
	●		●		●	
●	□	●	□	●	□	●
	●		●		●	

□   Color Block A
●   Color Block B
(Open)   Color Block C

Summer Woods

Snuggle up with a cup of cocoa as you keep warm with this richly colored, elegant afghan. The variety of stitches keeps you fascinated row after row — and you'll continue to admire the intricate details once you have completed the attractive afghan.

Design by Jane Campbell of Monroe City, Indiana

MATERIALS

- **Bulky weight yarn**
  -Sage Green   (35 oz, 1,628 yds)
- **Straight knitting needles, size U.S. 10½ (6.5 mm)**
- **36" circular knitting needle, size U.S. 10½ (6.5 mm)**
- **Crochet hook (optional), size K-10½ (6.5 mm)**
- **7 stitch holders**
- **Cable needle**
- **Tapestry needle**

PATTERN NOTES
- To yo before a purl st, bring yarn forward before wrapping around needle.
- Use the provisional cast-on method for all panels. This method is a temporary cast-on that is raveled later. (See "Provisional Cast-on" box below for details)

AFGHAN FINISHED SIZE
Approx 42" × 56"

STITCH GUIDE
cr 2 L: Sl 2 sts one at a time knitwise; then put the left needle through both, right to left, and sl them back to left needle; knit one at a time.

cr 2 R: Knit second st on left needle (passing in front of first st); knit the first st; let both sl off left needle.

inc: Knit in front lp then back lp of st.

kpk: Knit, purl, and knit again in same st.

M1 (make 1): Insert left needle, front to back, into strand bet needles; knit the lifted strand through back lp.

AFGHAN GAUGE
12 sts and 18 rows = 4" in St st

p inc: Purl in front lp then back lp of st.

sl1k: Slip 1 knitwise.

sl2p: Slip 1 purlwise.

ssk: Sl 2 sts one at a time knitwise; insert left needle into front of these 2 slipped sts and knit them tog.

ssp: Sl 2 sts one at a time knitwise; slide both sts (now twisted) back to left needle; purl these 2 sts tog tbl, second st first.

tbl: Through back lp.

yb: Yarn back.

yf: Yarn forward.

PROVISIONAL CAST-ON
Method One: Using waste yarn, crochet a ch a few sts longer than you need. With your project yarn and knitting needle, pick up the number of sts listed in pat through the back bumps of each ch. Knit the rest of piece as directed. When you are ready to use the first row of sts, simply take out the last crochet lp and pull out ch. Your knitted lps are ready to pick up and knit.

Method Two: Using waste yarn, cast on number of sts listed in pat. Work 2-4 rows in waste yarn. Beg knitting the next row with project yarn. When you are finished with your knitted piece, go back and pick up the sts of the first row you knit with the project yarn. Cut the first st of waste yarn and ravel. Knit as instructed.

DIRECTIONS

SYCAMORE/BRAMBLES (CENTER) PANEL (MAKE 1)
With straight needles, cast on 28 sts.
Foundation Row (WS): K1, p8, k1, p2, k4, p2, k1, p8, k1.
- **Row 1:** P10, k2, p4, k2, p10.
- **Row 2:** K1, (p3tog, kpk) twice, k1, p2, k4, p2, k1, (kpk, p3tog) twice, k1.
- **Row 3:** Rep Row 1.
- **Row 4:** K1, (kpk, p3tog) twice, k1, yf, sl2p, yb, k4, yf, sl2k, yb, k1, (p3tog, kpk) twice, k1.

- **Row 5:** P10, sl 2 sts onto cable needle, hold in front of work, p2, yo, k2tog tbl from cable needle, sl 2 sts onto cable needle, hold in back of work, k2tog, yo, p2 from cable needle, p10.
- **Row 6:** K1, (p3tog, kpk) twice, k1, p2, yb, sl1k, slide back to left needle, k1, p2, k1 tbl, p2, k1, (kpk, p3tog) twice, k1.
- **Row 7:** Rep Row 1.
- **Row 8:** K1, (kpk, p3tog) twice, k1, p2, k4, p2, k1, (p3tog, kpk) twice, k1.

Rep Rows 1-8 twenty-seven times.

Rep Rows 1 and 2 again.

Final Row: P1, k8, p1, k2, p4, k2, p1, k8, p1.

Transfer sts to holder. Cut yarn.

RIGHT VINING LEAF PANEL (MAKE 1)

With straight needles, cast on 22 sts.

- **Row 1 (WS):** K10, p3, k9.
- **Row 2:** P7, p2tog, inc, k2, p10.
- **Row 3:** K10, p2, k1, p1, k8.
- **Row 4:** P6, p2tog, k1, p inc, k2, p10.
- **Row 5:** K10, p2, k2, p1, k7.
- **Row 6:** P5, p2tog, k1, p inc, p1, k2, p10.
- **Row 7:** K10, p2, k3, p1, k6.
- **Row 8:** P4, p2tog, k1, p inc, p2, k2, p10.
- **Row 9:** K10, p2, k4, p1, k5.
- **Row 10:** P5, (k1, yo, k1) in next st, p4, k2, p10.
- **Row 11:** K10, p2, k4, p3, k5.
- **Row 12:** P5, k1, (k1, yo, k1) in next st, k1, p4, k1, M1, k1, p2tog, p8.
- **Row 13:** K9, p3, k4, p5, k5.
- **Row 14:** P5, k2, (k1, yo, k1) in next st, k2, p4, k1, inc, k1, p2tog, p7.
- **Row 15:** K8, p1, k1, p2, k4, p7, k5.
- **Row 16:** P5, k3, (k1, yo, k1) in next st, k3, p4, k2, p inc, k1, p2tog, p6.
- **Row 17:** K7, p1, k2, p2, k4, p9, k5.
- **Row 18:** P5, ssk, k5, k2tog, p4, k2, p1, p inc, k1, p2tog, p5.
- **Row 19:** K6, p1, k3, p2, k4, p7, k5.
- **Row 20:** P5, ssk, k3, k2tog, p4, k2, p2, p inc, k1, p2tog, p4.
- **Row 21:** K5, p1, k4, p2, k4, p5, k5.
- **Row 22:** P5, ssk, k1, k2tog, p4, k2, p4, (k1, yo, k1) in next st, p5.
- **Row 23:** K5, p3, k4, p2, k4, p3, k5.
- **Row 24:** P5, sl1k, k2tog, psso, p2, p2tog, k1, M1, k1, p4, k1, (k1, yo, k1) in next st, k1, p5.
- **Row 25:** K5, p5, k4, p3, k9.

- **Row 26:** P7, p2tog, inc, k2, p4, k2, (k1, yo, k1) in next st, k2, p5.
- **Row 27:** K5, p7, k4, p2, k1, p1, k8.
- **Row 28:** P6, p2tog, k1, p inc, k2, p4, k3, (k1, yo, k1) in next st, k3, p5.
- **Row 29:** K5, p9, k4, p2, k2, p1, k7.
- **Row 30:** P5, p2tog, k1, p inc, p1, k2, p4, ssk, k5, k2tog, p5.
- **Row 31:** K5, p7, k4, p2, k3, p1, k6.
- **Row 32:** P4, p2tog, k1, p inc, p2, k2, p4, ssk, k3, k2tog, p5.
- **Row 33:** K5, p5, k4, p2, k4, p1, k5.
- **Row 34:** P5, (k1, yo, k1) in next st, p4, k2, p4, ssk, k1, k2tog, p5.
- **Row 35:** K5, p3, k4, p2, k4, p3, k5.
- **Row 36:** P5, k1, (k1, yo, k1) in next st, k1, p4, k1, M1, k1, p2tog, p2, sl1k, k2tog, psso, p5.

Rep Rows 13-36 seven times.

Rep Rows 13-23 again.

- **Row 216:** P5, sl1k, k2tog, psso, p4, k2, p4, k1, (k1, yo, k1) in next st, k1, p5.
- **Row 217:** K5, p5, k4, p2, k10.
- **Row 218:** P10, k2, p4, k2, (k1, yo, k1) in next st, k2, p5.
- **Row 219:** K5, p7, k4, p2, k10.
- **Row 220:** P10, k2, p4, k3, (k1, yo, k1) in next st, k3, p5.
- **Row 221:** K5, p9, k4, p2, k10.
- **Row 222:** P10, k2, p4, ssk, k5, k2tog, p5.
- **Row 223:** K5, p7, k4, p2, k10.
- **Row 224:** P10, k2, p4, ssk, k3, k2tog, p5.
- **Row 225:** K5, p5, k4, p2, k10.
- **Row 226:** P10, k2, p4, ssk, k1, k2tog, p5.
- **Row 227:** K5, p3, k4, p2, k10.
- **Row 228:** P10, k2, p4, sl1k, k2tog, psso, p5.

Transfer sts to holder. Cut yarn.

LEFT VINING LEAF PANEL (MAKE 1)

With straight needles, cast on 22 sts.

- **Row 1 (WS):** K9, p3, k10.
- **Row 2:** P10, k1, inc, k1, p2tog, p7.
- **Row 3:** K8, p1, k1, p2, k10.
- **Row 4:** P10, k2, p inc, k1, p2tog, p6.
- **Row 5:** K7, p1, k2, p2, k10.
- **Row 6:** P10, k2, p1, p inc, k1, p2tog, p5.
- **Row 7:** K6, p1, k3, p2, k10.
- **Row 8:** P10, k2, p2, p inc, k1, p2tog, p4.
- **Row 9:** K5, p1, k4, p2, k10.
- **Row 10:** P10, k2, p4, (k1, yo, k1) in next st, p5.
- **Row 11:** K5, p3, k4, p2, k10.
- **Row 12:** P8, p2tog, k1, M1, k1, p4, k1, (k1, yo, k1) in next st, k1, p5.

- **Rows 13-24:** Rep Rows 25-36 of Right Panel.

Rep Rows 13-36 of Right Panel seven times.

Rep Rows 13-35 of Right Panel again.

- **Row 216:** P5, k1, (k1, yo, k1) in next st, k1, p4, k2, p4, sl1k, k2tog, psso, p5.
- **Row 217:** K10, p2, k4, p5, k5.
- **Row 218:** P5, k2, (k1, yo, k1) in next st, k2, p4, k2, p10.
- **Row 219:** K10, p2, k4, p7, k5.
- **Row 220:** P5, k3, (k1, yo, k1) in next st, k3, p4, k2, p10.
- **Row 221:** K10, p2, k4, p9, k5.
- **Row 222:** P5, ssk, k5, k2tog, p4, k2, p10.
- **Row 223:** K10, p2, k4, p7, k5.
- **Row 224:** P5, ssk, k3, k2tog, p4, k2, p10.
- **Row 225:** K10, p2, k4, p5, k5.
- **Row 226:** P5, ssk, k1, k2tog, p4, k2, p10.
- **Row 227:** K10, p2, k4, p3, k5.
- **Row 228:** P5, sl1k, k2tog, psso, p4, k2, p10.

Transfer sts to holder. Cut yarn.

ACORN ON MOSS PANEL (MAKE 2)

With straight needles, cast on 19 sts.

- **Row 1 (RS):** K2, (p1, k1) 3 times, (k1, yo) twice, k1, (k1, p1) 3 times, k2. (21 sts)
- **Row 2:** P1, (p1, k1) 3 times, ssp, p3, p2tog, (k1, p1) 3 times, p1. (19 sts)
- **Row 3:** (K1, p1) 3 times, k2, yo, k3, yo, k2, (p1, k1) 3 times. (21 sts)
- **Row 4:** (P1, k1) 3 times, ssp, p5, p2tog, (k1, p1) 3 times. (19 sts)
- **Row 5:** K2, (p1, k1) twice, p1, yo, k5, yo, p1, (k1, p1) twice, k2. (21 sts)
- **Row 6:** P1, (p1, k1) 3 times, p7, (k1, p1) 3 times, p1. (21 sts)
- **Row 7:** K1, (p1, k1) 3 times, p7, (k1, p1) 3 times, k1. (21 sts)
- **Row 8:** P1, (k1, p1) 3 times, yo, ssk, k3, k2tog, yo, (p1, k1) 3 times, p1. (21 sts)
- **Row 9:** K2, (p1, k1) 3 times, p5, (k1, p1) 3 times, k2. (21 sts)
- **Row 10:** P2, (k1, p1) 3 times, yo, ssk, k1, k2tog, yo, (p1, k1) 3 times, p2. (21 sts)
- **Row 11:** K1, (p1, k1) 4 times, p3, (k1, p1) 4 times, k1. (21 sts)
- **Row 12:** P1, (k1, p1) 4 times, sl2tog knitwise, k1, p2sso, (k1, p1) 4 times, p1. (19 sts)

Rep Rows 1-12 eighteen times.

Transfer sts to holder. Cut yarn.

RIGHT TWIG PANEL (MAKE 1)

With straight needles, cast on 18 sts.

- **Rows 1, 3, and 5 (WS):** P14, k4.
- **Row 2:** K3, p1, k6, cr 2 L, k6.
- **Row 4:** K3, p1, k7, cr 2 L, k5.

- **Row 6:** K3, p1, k5, cr 2 R, k1, cr 2 L, k4.
- **Row 7 and All Odd Rows:** P14, k4.
- **Row 8:** K3, p1, k4, cr 2 R, k3, cr 2 L, k3.
- **Row 10:** K3, p1, k3, cr 2 R, k1, cr 2 L, k2, cr 2 L, k2.
- **Row 12:** K3, p1, k2, cr 2 R, k3, cr 2 L, k5.
- **Row 14:** K3, p1, k1, cr 2 R, k2, cr 2 R, k1, cr 2 L, k4.

Rep Rows 7-14 twenty-six times.

Rep Rows 7-12 again.

Transfer sts to holder. Cut yarn.

LEFT TWIG PANEL (MAKE 1)

With straight needles, cast on 18 sts.

- **Rows 1, 3 and 5 (WS):** K4, p14.
- **Row 2:** K6, cr 2 R, k6, p1, k3.
- **Row 4:** K5, cr 2 R, k7, p1, k3.
- **Row 6:** K4, cr 2 R, k1, cr 2 L, k5, p1, k3.
- **Row 7 and All Odd Rows:** K4, p14.
- **Row 8:** K3, cr 2 R, k3, cr 2 L, k4, p1, k3.
- **Row 10:** K2, cr 2 R, k2, cr 2 R, k1, cr 2 L, k3, p1, k3.
- **Row 12:** K5, cr 2 R, k3, cr 2 L, k2, p1, k3.
- **Row 14:** K4, cr 2 R, k1, cr 2 L, k2, cr 2 L, k1, p1, k3.

Rep Rows 7-14 twenty-six times.

Rep Rows 7-12 again.

Transfer sts to holder.

Do not cut yarn (will be used for top border).

FINISHING

With RS of panels tog, sew panel seams 1 st in from edge in following order, from left to right:

1. Left Twig
2. Acorn on Moss
3. Left Vining Leaf
4. Sycamore/Brambles
5. Right Vining Leaf
6. Acorn on Moss
7. Right Twig

TOP BORDER

Transfer sts from holders onto circular needle. (146 sts)

- **Row 1 (WS):** Knit across, dec at seams by k2tog on RS of seam and ssk on left side. Also dec on center 10 sts of the Sycamore cable as follows: K2, k2tog, k2, ssk, k2. (132 sts)
- **Rows 2-5:** Knit across.

BO loosely.

BOTTOM BORDER

Transfer provisional cast-on sts to circular needle.

- **Row 1 (RS):** Knit across, working decs to correspond to top border.
- **Rows 2-6:** Knit across.

BO loosely. ❖

Lilac Fantasy
This romantic, delicate afghan will capture your heart. The combination of cables, textured stitches, and embellishments will have you enjoying the knitting every stitch of the way.

Design by Georgia Vincent of Dowboro, New Hampshire

AFGHAN FINISHED SIZE
Approx 46" × 60", not including fringe

AFGHAN GAUGE
16 sts = 4" in St st

STITCH GUIDE

kp: Knit, purl, both in same st.

kpk: Knit, purl, knit all in same st.

kyo: Knit the yarn over.

k2togB: Knit 2 sts together through the back lp.

skpo: With yarn in back, sl 1, k1, psso. (1 dec)

skpo-sbpo: Sl 1, k1, pass first st over second, then sl this st just made back to the left needle; pass the second st on the left needle over this slipped st and sl the st back to the right needle. (2 sts dec)

BC (Baby Cable): Knit second st on left needle, do not remove from needle; knit first st on left needle, transfer both sts to right needle.

C6B (Cable 6 Back): Transfer next 3 sts to cable needle, place at back of work; knit next 3 sts on left needle, knit 3 sts from cable needle, being careful not to twist your sts.

C6F (Cable 6 Front): Transfer next 3 sts to cable needle, place at front of work; knit next 3 sts on left needle, knit 3 sts from cable needle, being careful not to twist your sts.

sl1k: Slip 1 knitwise.

MATERIALS

- **4-ply worsted weight yarn**
  - Lilac (56 oz, 2,608 yds)
  - White (3½ oz, 163 yds)
  - Light Pink (3½ oz, 163 yds)
  - Light Blue (3½ oz, 163 yds)
  - Light Yellow (3½ oz, 163 yds)
  - Light Green (3½ oz, 163 yds)
- **Soft 4-ply worsted weight yarn**
  - Dark Lilac (3½ oz, 195 yds)
- **14" straight knitting needles, sizes U.S. 9 (5.5 mm), U.S. 6 (4.0 mm), and U.S. 4 (3.5 mm) or sizes to obtain gauge**
- **Crochet hook, size F-5 (3.75 mm), to attach fringe**
- **Cable needle**
- **Tapestry needle**
- **2 yds ¼"-wide light orchid ribbon**

PATTERN NOTES

- Before doing the (yo, sl yo, p2) in Row 4 of the side panel (and after the p1 before it), bring yarn to the back as if to knit. Bring yarn over the top of the right needle and forward to do the yo. When you sl the yo from the previous row the two yos will tend to cross. This is OK and will make it easier to identify these two yos as the ones to be knit tog in Row 5.

- To do the (k1, kyo, k under both lps of yos, k1) in Row 5 of the side panel, k1, k1 in the back lp of the first yo, leaving it on the left needle; knit the two lps that cross, pushing both sts off left needle, then k1.

DIRECTIONS

SIDE PANEL (MAKE 2)

With Lilac and size 9 needles, cast on 72 sts.

- **Row 1:** K1, p1, k4, p2, k6, yo, k1, yo, k6, p2, k4, p1, k16, p1, k4, p2, k6, yo, k1, yo, k6, p2, k4, p1, k1. (76 sts)
- **Row 2:** (K2, p1) twice, k2, p6, p3tog, p6, (k2, p1) twice, k1, p16, k1, (p1, k2) twice, p6, p3tog, p6, k2, (p1, k2) twice. (72 sts)

- **Row 3:** K1, p1, k4, p2, C6B, yo, k1, yo, C6F, p2, k4, p1, (k2tog, yo, k2togB) 4 times, p1, k4, p2, C6B yo, k1, yo, C6F, p2, k4, p1, k1. (72 sts)
- **Row 4:** (K2, p1) twice, k2, p6, p3tog, p6, (k2, p1) twice, k1, p1, (yo, sl yo, p2) 3 times, yo, sl yo, p1, k1, (p1, k2) twice, p6, p3tog, p6, (k2, p1) twice, k2. (72 sts)
- **Row 5:** K1, p1, k4, p2, k6, yo, k1, yo, k6, p2, k4, p1, (k1, kyo, knit under both lps of yos to create hole,

k1) 4 times, p1, k4, p2, k6, yo, k1, yo, k6, p2, k4, p1, k1. (76 sts)

- **Row 6:** Rep Row 2. (72 sts)
- **Row 7:** K1, p1, k4, p2, k6, yo, k1, yo, k6, p2, k4, p1, knit in back of second st on needle, then in front of first st, (k2tog, yo, k2togB) 3 times, knit second st on needle, then knit first, p1, k4, p2, k6, yo, k1, yo, k6, p2, k4, p1, k1. (73 sts)
- **Row 8:** (K2, p1) twice, k2, p6, p3tog, p6, (k2, p1) twice, k1, p3, (yo, sl yo, p2) 3 times, p1, k1, (p1, k2) twice, p6, p3tog, p6, k2, (p1, k2) twice. (72 sts)
- **Row 9:** K1, p1, k4, p2, k6, yo, k1, yo, k6, p2, k4, p1, k3, (kyo, k under both lps of yos, k2) 3 times, k1, p1, k4, p2, k6, yo, k1, yo, k6, p2, k4, p1, k1. (76 sts)
- **Row 10:** Rep Row 2. (72 sts)

Rep Rows 3-10 thirty-eight times.
Rep Rows 3-4 once. BO.

CENTER PANEL

Note: The number of sts in each row changes in this part of the pattern. With Lilac and size 9 needles, cast on 75 sts.

FOUNDATION ROWS

- **Row 1:** K1, p1, k4, p2, BC, p11, BC, p2, k4, p2, k6, yo, k1, yo, k6, p2, k4, p2, BC, p11, BC, p2, k4, p1, k1. (77 sts)
- **Row 2:** (K2, p1) twice, k2, p2, k1, (kpk, p3tog) twice, kpk, k1, p2, (k2, p1) twice, k2, p6, p3tog, p6, k2, (p1, k2) twice, p2, k1, (kpk, p3tog) twice, kpk, k1, p2, k2, (p1, k2) twice. (79 sts)

CENTER PANEL PATTERN

- **Row 1:** K1, p1, k4, p2, BC, p13, BC, p2, k4, p2, C6B, yo k1, yo, C6F, p2, k4, p2, BC, p13, BC, p2, k4, p1, k1. (81 sts)
- **Row 2:** (K2, p1) twice, k2, p2, k1, (p3tog, kpk) twice, p3tog, k1, p2, (k2, p1) twice, k2, p6, p3tog, p6, k2, (p1, k2) twice, p2, k1, p3tog, (kpk, p3tog) twice, k1, p2, k2, (p1, k2) twice. (75 sts)
- **Row 3:** K1, p1, k4, p2, BC, p11, BC, p2, k4, p2, k6, yo, k1, yo, k6, p2, k4, p2, BC, p11, BC, p2, k4, p1, k1. (77 sts)
- **Row 4:** (K2, p1) twice, k2, p2, k1, (kpk, p3tog) twice, kpk, k1, p2, (k2, p1) twice, k2, p6, p3tog, p6, k2, (p1, k2) twice, p2, k1, kpk, (p3tog, kpk) twice, k1, p2, k2, (p1, k2) twice. (79 sts)
- **Row 5:** K1, p1, k4, p2, BC, p13, BC, p2, k4, p2, k6, yo, k1, yo, k6, p2, k4, p2, BC, p13, BC, p2, k4, p1, k1. (81 sts)
- **Row 6:** Rep Row 2.
- **Row 7:** Rep Row 3.
- **Row 8:** Rep Row 4.

Rep Rows 1-8 six times.

Rep Rows 1-4 once more.

CENTER DESIGN

- **Row 1:** K1, p1, k4, p2, BC, p13, BC, p2, k4, p2, k5, p3, k5, p2, k4, p2, BC, p13, BC, p2, k4, p1, k1. (79 sts)
- **Row 2:** (K2, p1) twice, k2, p2, k1, (p3tog, kpk) twice, p3tog, k1, p2, (k2, p1) twice, k2, p4, k5, p4, k2, (p1, k2) twice, p2, k1, p3tog, (kpk, p3tog) twice, k1, p2, k2, (p1, k2) twice. (75 sts)
- **Row 3:** K1, p1, k4, p2, BC, p11, BC, p2, k4, p2, k2, p2tog, p1, k3, p1, p2tog, k2, p2, k4, p2, BC, p11, BC, p2, k4, p1, k1. (73 sts)
- **Row 4:** (K2, p1) twice, k2, p2, k1, (kpk, p3tog) twice, kpk, k1, p2, (k2, p1) twice, k2, p1, k2, p5, k2, p1, k2, (p1, k2) twice, p2, k1, kpk, (p3tog, kpk) twice, k1, p2, k2, (p1, k2) twice. (77 sts)
- **Row 5:** K1, p1, k4, p2, BC, p13, BC, p2, k4, p4, k1, p1, k3, p1, k1, p4, k4, p2, BC, p13, BC, p2, k4, p1, k1. (77 sts)
- **Row 6:** (K2, p1) twice, k2, p2, k1, (p3tog, kpk) twice, p3tog, k1, p2, (k2, p1) twice, k2tog, k1, p3, k1, p1, k1, p3, k1, k2tog, (p1, k2) twice, p2, k1, p3tog, (kpk, p3tog) twice, k1, p2, k2, (p1, k2) twice. (71 sts)
- **Row 7:** K1, p1, k4, p2, BC, p11, BC, p2, k3, p2, k5, p1, k5, p2, k3, p2, BC, p11, BC, p2, k4, p1, k1. (71 sts)
- **Row 8:** (K2, p1) twice, k2, p2, k1, (kpk, p3tog) twice, kpk, k1, p2, k2, p1, k3, p1, k1, p3, k1, p1, k1, p3, k1, p1, k3, p1, k2, p2, k1, kpk, (p3tog, kpk) twice, k1, p2, k2, (p1, k2) twice. (75 sts)
- **Row 9:** K1, p1, k4, p2, BC, p13, BC, p2, k1, p2, (k3, p1, k1, p1) twice, k3, p2, k1, p2, BC, p13, BC, p2, k4, p1, k1. (75 sts)
- **Row 10:** (K2, p1) twice, k2, p2, k1, (p3tog, kpk) twice, p3tog, k1, p2, k4, p5, (k1, p5) twice, k4, p2, k1, p3tog, (kpk, p3tog) twice, k1, p2, k2, (p1, k2) twice. (71 sts)
- **Row 11:** K1, p1, k4, p2, BC, p11, BC, p2tog, (p1, k1, p1, k3) 3 times, p1, k1, p1, p2tog, BC, p11, BC, p2, k4, p1, k1. (69 sts)
- **Row 12:** (K2, p1) twice, k2, p2, k1, (kpk, p3tog) twice, kpk, k1, p1, k2, (p3, k1, p1, k1) 3 times, p3, k2, p1, k1, kpk, (p3tog, kpk) twice, k1, p2, k2, (p1, k2) twice. (73 sts)
- **Row 13:** K1, p1, k4, p2, BC, p12, k1, p2, (k5, p1) 3 times, k5, p2, k1, p12, BC, p2 k4, p1, k1. (73 sts)
- **Row 14:** (K2, p1) twice, k2, p2, k1, (p3tog, kpk) twice, p3tog, k2, p1, k1, (p3, k1, p1, k1) 3 times, p3, k1, p1, k2, p3tog, (kpk, p3tog) twice, k1, p2, k2, (p1, k2) twice. (69 sts)
- **Row 15:** K1, p1, k4, p2, BC, p11, (k3, p1, k1, p1) 4 times, k3, p11, BC, p2, k4, p1, k1. (69 sts)

Note: At this point, recheck your gauge. Your afghan should measure 46½" wide. If it does not, start over with a smaller or larger needle.

- **Row 16:** (K2, p1) twice, k2, p2, k1, kpk, p3tog, kpk, p2tog, k2, (p5, k1) 4 times, p5, k2, p2tog, kpk, p3tog, kpk, k1, p2, k2, (p1, k2) twice. (71 sts)
- **Row 17:** K1, p1, k4, p2, BC, p10, k1, p1, (k3, p1, k1, p1) 4 times, k3, p1, k1, p10, BC, p2, k4, p1, k1. (71 sts)
- **Row 18:** (K2, p1) twice, k2, p2, k1, p3tog, kpk, p2tog, k2, (p3, k1, p1, k1) 5 times, p3, k2, p2tog, kpk, p3tog, k1, p2, k2, (p1, k2) twice. (69 sts)
- **Row 19:** K1, p1, k4, p2, BC, p7, (k5, p1) 5 times, k5, p7, BC, p2, k4, p1, k1. (69 sts)
- **Row 20:** (K2, p1) twice, k2, p2, k1, kpk, p2tog, k2, p1, k1, (p3, k1, p1, k1) 5 times, p3, k1, p1, k2, p2tog, kpk, k1, p2, k2, (p1, k2) twice. (71 sts)
- **Row 21:** K1, p1, k4, p2, BC, p6, (k3, p1, k1, p1) 6 times, k3, p6, BC, p2, k4, p1, k1. (71 sts)
- **Row 22:** (K2, p1) twice, k2, p2, k1, p2tog, k2, (p5, k1) 6 times, p5, k2, p2tog, k1, p2, k2, (p1, k2) twice. (69 sts)
- **Row 23:** K1, p1, k4, p2, BC, p2tog, (p1, k1, p1, k3) 7 times, p1, k1, p1, p2tog, BC, p2, k4, p1, k1. (67 sts)
- **Row 24:** (K2, p1) 3 times, k2, (p3, k1, p1, k1) 7 times, p3, k2, (p1, k2) 3 times. (67 sts)
- **Row 25:** K1, p1, k4, p4, (k5, p1) 7 times, k5, p4, k4, p1, k1. (67 sts)
- **Row 26:** (K2, p1) twice, k2tog, p2, k1, (p3, k1, p1, k1) 7 times, p3, k1, p2, k2tog, (p1, k2) twice. (65 sts)
- **Row 27:** K1, p1, k4, p1, (k3, p1, k1, p1) 8 times, k3, p1, k4, p1, k1. (65 sts)
- **Row 28:** (K2, p1) twice, k1, p4, (k1, p5) 8 times, k1, p4, k1, (p1, k2) twice. (71 sts)
- **Row 29:** K1, p1, k4, p1, (k3, p1, k1, p1) 8 times, k3, p1, k4, p1, k1. (65 sts)
- **Row 30:** (K2, p1) twice, k1, p2, k1, (p3, k1, p1, k1) 7 times, p3, k1, p2, k1, (p1, k2) twice. (65 sts)
- **Row 31:** K1, p1, k4, p1, k1, (p1, k5) 8 times, p1, k1, p1, k4, p1, k1. (65 sts)
- **Row 32:** (K2, p1) twice, k1, p2, k1, (p3, k1, p1, k1) 7 times, p3, k1, p2, k1, (p1, k2) twice. (65 sts)
- **Row 33:** K1, p1, k4, p1, (k3, p1, k1, p1) 8 times, k3, p1, k4, p1, k1. (65 sts)
- **Row 34:** (K2, p1) twice, k1, p4, (k1, p5) 7 times, k1, p4, k1, (p1, k2) twice. (65 sts)

Rep Rows 29-34 twenty-one times.

CLOSE CENTER DESIGN

- **Row 1:** K1, p1, k4, p1, (k3, p1, k1, p1) 8 times, k3, p1, k4, p1, k1. (65 sts)
- **Row 2:** (K2, p1) twice, inc in next st, p2, k1, (p3, k1, p1, k1) 7 times, p3, k1, p2, inc in next st, (p1, k2) twice. (67 sts)
- **Row 3:** K1, p1, k4, p4, (k5, p1) 7 times, k5, p4, k4, p1, k1. (67 sts)

- **Row 4:** (K2, p1) 3 times, k2, (p3, k1, p1, k1) 7 times, p3, k2, (p1, k2) 3 times. (67 sts)
- **Row 5:** K1, p1, k4, p2, BC, inc in next st, (p1, k1, p1, k3) 7 times, p1, k1, p1, inc in next st, BC, p2, k4, p1, k1. (69 sts)
- **Row 6:** (K2, p1) twice, k2, p2, k1, kp, k2, (p5, k1) 6 times, p5, k2 kp, k1, p2, k2, (p1, k2) twice. (71 sts)
- **Row 7:** K1, p1, k4, p2, BC, p6, (k3, p1, k1, p1) 6 times, k3, p6, BC, p2, k4, p1, k1. (71 sts)
- **Row 8:** (K2, p1) twice, k2, p2, k1, p3tog, kpk, k2, p1, k1, (p3, k1, p1, k1) 5 times, p3, k1, p1, k2, kpk, p3tog, k1, p2, k2, (p1, k2) twice. (71 sts)
- **Row 9:** K1, p1, k4, p2, BC, p5, p2tog, p1, (k5, p1) 6 times, p2tog, p5, BC, p2, k4, p1, k1. (69 sts)
- **Row 10:** (K2, p1) twice, k2, p2, k1, kpk, p3tog, kpk, k2, (p3, k1, p1, k1) 5 times, p3, k2, kpk, p3tog, kpk, k1, p2, k2, (p1, k2) twice. (73 sts)
- **Row 11:** K1, p1, k4, p2, BC, p8, p2tog, p1, k1, p1, (k3, p1, k1, p1) 5 times, p2tog, p8, BC, p2, k4, p1, k1. (71 sts)
- **Row 12:** (K2, p1) twice, k2, p2, k1, (p3tog, kpk) twice, k2, (p5, k1) 4 times, p5, k2, (kpk, p3tog) twice, k1, p2, k2, (p1, k2) twice. (71 sts)
- **Row 13:** K1, p1, k4, p2, BC, p9, p2tog, p1, (k3, p1, k1, p1) 4 times, k3, p1, p2tog, p9, BC, p2, k4, p1, k1. (69 sts)
- **Row 14:** (K2, p1) twice, k2, p2, k1, (kpk, p3tog) twice, kpk, k2, p1, k1, (p3, k1, p1, k1) 3 times, p3, k1, p1, k2, kpk, (p3tog, kpk) twice, k1, p2, k2, (p1, k2) twice. (73 sts)
- **Row 15:** K1, p1, k4, p2, BC, p12, p2tog, p1, (k5, p1) 4 times, p2tog, p12, BC, p2, k4, p1, k1. (71 sts)
- **Row 16:** (K2, p1) twice, k2, p2, k1, (p3tog, kpk) twice, p3tog, k3, (p3, k1, p1, k1) 3 times, p3, k3, p3tog, (kpk, p3tog) twice, k1, p2, k2, (p1, k2) twice. (67 sts)
- **Row 17:** K1, p1, k4, p2, BC, p11, inc in next st, p2, k1, p1, (k3, p1, k1, p1) twice, k3, p1, k1, p2, inc in next st, p11, BC, p2, k4, p1, k1. (69 sts)
- **Row 18:** (K2, p1) twice, k2, p2, k1, (kpk, p3tog) twice, kpk, k1, p2, k3, (p5, k1) twice, p5, k3, p2, k1, kpk, (p3tog, kpk) twice, k1, p2, k2, (p1, k2) twice. (73 sts)
- **Row 19:** K1, p1, k4, p2, BC, p13, BC, p4, (k3, p1, k1, p1) twice, k3, p4, BC, p13, BC, p2, k4, p1, k1. (73 sts)
- **Row 20:** (K2, p1) twice, k2, p2, k1, (p3tog, kpk) twice, p3tog, k1, p2, (k2, p1) twice, k1, p3, k1, p1, k1, p3, k1, (p1, k2) twice, p2, k1, p3tog, (kpk, p3tog) twice, k1, p2, k2, (p1, k2) twice. (69 sts)
- **Row 21:** K1, p1, k4, p2, BC, p11, BC, p2, k2, p2, k5, p1, k5, p2, k2, p2, BC, p11, BC, p2, k4, p1, k1. (69 sts)

- **Row 22:** (K2, p1) twice, k2, p2, k1, (kpk, p3tog) twice, kpk, k1, p2, k2, p1, k1, inc in next st, k2, p3, k1, p1, k1, p3, k2, inc in next st, k1, p1, k2, p2, k1, kpk, (p3tog, kpk) twice, k1, p2, k2, (p1, k2) twice. (75 sts)
- **Row 23:** K1, p1, k4, p2, BC, p13, BC, p2, k4, p3, k1, p1, k3, p1, k1, p3, k4, p2, BC, p13, BC, p2, k4, p1, k1. (75 sts)
- **Row 24:** (K2, p1) twice, k2, p2, k1, (p3tog, kpk) twice, p3tog, k1, p2, (k2, p1) twice, k1, inc in next st, k2, p5, k2, inc in next st, k1, (p1, k2) twice, p2, k1, p3tog, (kpk, p3tog) twice, k1, p2, k2, (p1, k2) twice. (73 sts)
- **Row 25:** K1, p1, k4, p2, BC, p11, BC, p2, k4, p2, k2, p2, k3, p2, k2, p2, k4, p2, BC, p11, BC, p2, k4, p1, k1. (73 sts)
- **Row 26:** (K2, p1) twice, k2, p2, k1, (kpk, p3tog) twice, kpk, k1, p2, (k2, p1) twice, k2, p3, k2, p1, k2, p3, k2, (p1, k2) twice, p2, k1, kpk, (p3tog, kpk) twice, k1, p2, k2, (p1, k2) twice. (77 sts)
- **Row 27:** K1, p1, k4, p2, BC, p13, BC, p2, k4, p2, k2, inc in next st, k1, p3, k1, inc in next st, k2, p2, k4, p2, BC, p13, BC, p2, k4, p1, k1. (79 sts)
- **Row 28:** (K2, p1) twice, k2, p2, k1, (p3tog, kpk) twice, p3tog, k1, p2, (k2, p1) twice, k2, p6, k1, p6, k2, (p1, k2) twice, p2, k1, p3tog, (kpk, p3tog) twice, k1, p2, k2, (p1, k2) twice. (75 sts)
- **Row 29:** K1, p1, k4, p2, BC, p11, BC, p2, k4, p2, k6, yo, k1, yo, k6, p2, k4, p2, BC, p11, BC, p2, k4, p1, k1. (77 sts)
- **Row 30:** (K2, p1) twice, k2, p2, k1, (kpk, p3tog) twice, kpk, k1, p2, (k2, p1) twice, k2, p6, p3tog, p6, k2, (p1, k2) twice, p2, k1, kpk, (p3tog, kpk) twice, k1, p2, k2, (p1, k2) twice. (79 sts)
- **Row 31:** K1, p1, k4, p2, BC, p13, BC, p2, k4, p2, k6, yo, k1, yo, k6, p2, k4, p2, BC, p13, BC, p2, k4, p1, k1. (81 sts)
- **Row 32:** (K2, p1) twice, k2, p2, k1, (p3tog, kpk) twice, p3tog, k1, p2, (k2, p1) twice, k2, p6, p3tog, p6, k2, (p1, k2) twice, p2, k1, p3tog, (kpk, p3tog) twice, k1, p2, k2, (p1, k2) twice. (75 sts)
- **Row 33:** K1, p1, k4, p2, BC, p11, BC, p2, k4, p2, k6, yo, k1, yo, k6, p2, k4, p2, BC, p11, BC, p2, k4, p1, k1. (77 sts)
- **Row 34:** (K2, p1) twice, k2, p2, k1, (kpk, p3tog) twice, kpk, k1, p2, (k2, p1) twice, k2, p6, p3tog, p6, k2, (p1, k2) twice, p2, k1, kpk, (p3tog, kpk) twice, k1, p2, k2, (p1, k2) twice. (79 sts)

CLOSING CABLE PATTERN

- **Row 1:** K1, p1, k4, p2, BC, p13, BC, p2, k4, p2, C6F, yo, k1, yo, C6B, p2, k4, p2, BC, p13, BC, p2, k4, p1, k1. (81 sts)
- **Row 2:** (K2, p1) twice, k2, p2, k1, (p3tog, kpk) twice, p3tog, k1, p2, (k2, p1) twice, k2, p6, p3tog, p6, k2, (p1, k2) twice, p2, k1, p3tog, (kpk, p3tog) twice, k1, p2, k2, (p1, k2) twice. (75 sts)

- **Row 3:** K1, p1, k4, p2, BC, p11, BC, p2, k4, p2, k6, yo, k1, yo, k6, p2, k4, p2, BC, p11, BC, p2, k4, p1, k1. (77 sts)
- **Row 4:** (K2, p1) twice, k2, p2, k1, (kpk, p3tog) twice, kpk, k1, p2, (k2, p1) twice, k2, p6, p3tog, p6, k2, (p1, k2) twice, p2, k1, kpk, (p3tog, kpk) twice, k1, p2, k2, (p1, k2) twice. (79 sts)
- **Row 5:** K1, p1, k4, p2, BC, p13, BC, p2, k4, p2, k6, yo, k1, yo, k6, p2, k4, p2, BC, p13, BC, p2, k4, p1, k1. (81 sts)
- **Row 6:** (K2, p1) twice, k2, p2, k1, (p3tog, kpk) twice, p3tog, k1, p2, (k2, p1) twice, k2, p6, p3tog, p6, k2, (p1, k2) twice, p2, k1, p3tog, (kpk, p3tog) twice, k1, p2, k2, (p1, k2) twice. (75 sts)
- **Row 7:** K1, p1, k4, p2, BC, p11, BC, p2, k4, p2, k6, yo, k1, yo, k6, p2, k4, p2, BC, p11, BC, p2, k4, p1, k1. (77 sts)
- **Row 8:** (K2, p1) twice, k2, p2, k1, (kpk, p3tog) twice, kpk, k1, p2, (k2, p1) twice, k2, p6, p3tog, p6, k2, (p1, k2) twice, p2, k1, kpk, (p3tog, kpk) twice, k1, p2, k2, (p1, k2) twice. (79 sts)

Rep these 8 rows 6 times.

Rep Rows 1-4 once. BO.

EMBELLISHMENTS

FAN (MAKE 2)

With White and size 6 needles, loosely cast on 70 sts.

- **Row 1 (WS):** (Sl 1, p5, sl 1, yo) across to last 7 sts, sl 1, p5, sl 1. (79 sts)
- **Row 2:** (K2, sl1k, k2tog and psso, k2, yo wrapping yarn around needle twice, sl yo) across to last 7 sts, k2, sl1k, k2tog, psso, k2. (68 sts, counting double wrap yo as one st)
- **Row 3:** (P1, BO next 3 sts, sl 2 yos dropping extra wrap, yo wrapping yarn twice) across to last 5 sts, p1, BO 3 sts. (47 sts, counting double wrap yo as one st)
- **Row 4:** (K2tog, yo, k3 yos tog dropping extra wrap, yo) across to last 2 sts, k2tog. (37 sts)
- **Row 5:** (P1, yo, sl yo) across, end p1. (55 sts)
- **Row 6:** (K1, kyo, k under both lps of next yo) across, ending k1. (55 sts)
- **Row 7:** P1, p2tog, * p4, p2tog; rep from * across, ending p4. (46 sts)
- **Row 8:** Purl across.
- **Row 9:** P1, * yo, p2tog; rep from * across, ending yo, p1. Pick up 3 sts along side of last 3 rows. (50 sts)
- **Row 10:** Purl across. Pick up 3 sts along side of last 3 rows. (53 sts)
- **Row 11:** (P3, p2tog) across, ending p3. (43 sts)

- **Row 12:** K2, * yo, skpo-sbpo, yo, k1; rep from * across, ending k2 instead of k1. (43 sts)
- **Row 13:** Purl across.
- **Row 14:** K4, * yo, skpo-sbpo, yo, k1; rep from * across, ending k4 instead of k1. (43 sts)
- **Row 15:** Purl across.
- **Row 16:** Rep Row 12.
- **Row 17:** Purl across.
- **Row 18:** Rep Row 14.
- **Row 19:** (P3, p2tog) across, ending p3. (35 sts)
- **Row 20:** Purl across.
- **Row 21:** Purl across.
- **Row 22:** K1, * k1, p1; rep from * across, ending k2.
- **Row 23:** P1, * p1, k1; rep from * across, ending p2.
- **Rows 24-27:** Rep Rows 22-23 twice.
- **Row 28:** K2, k2tog across, ending k1. (19 sts)
- **Row 29:** Purl across.
- **Row 30:** Knit across.
- **Row 31:** Purl across.
- **Row 32:** K1, k2tog across to last 2 sts, k2. (11 sts)
- **Row 33:** Purl across.
- **Row 34:** Knit across.
- **Row 35:** Purl across.
- **Row 36:** K2tog across, ending k1. (6 sts)

BO leaving an end long enough to sew fan to afghan. Weave ribbon through yos in Row 9, tacking ends on WS. Make ribbon bows, one for each fan, and attach them to the base of each fan.

The colors and numbers of leaves and flowers are a matter of choice. Make them as shown in the photo or create your own arrangement to "tie" the two fans tog.

LEAVES

With Light Green and size 4 needles, cast on 3 sts.
- **Row 1 (WS):** P3.
- **Row 2:** K1, yo, k1, yo, k1.
- **Rows 3-11:** Purl across.
- **Row 4:** K2, yo, k1, yo, k2.
- **Row 6:** Knit across.
- **Row 8:** Skpo, k3, k2tog.
- **Row 10:** Skpo, k1, k2tog.
- **Row 12:** Skpo-sbpo, end off, leaving yarn end long enough to sew leaf to afghan. To make smaller leaves if desired, omit Rows 3-4 and Rows 7-8.

FLOWER 1

With Light Yellow and size 4 needles, cast on 41 sts.
- **Row 1:** (Sl 1, skpo-sbpo, k2tog) across, ending sl 1.

- **Row 2:** (Sl 1, skpo-sbpo) across, ending sl 1.

Cut length of yarn long enough to sew flower to blanket, thread it through tapestry needle, and run through lps on the knitting needle, pull tight and fasten off.

FLOWER 2

With Light Pink and size 4 needles, cast on 37 sts.
- **Row 1:** Sl first st, * BO 3 sts, sl 1, psso, sl this st back to left needle and k2tog; rep from * 5 times.
- **Row 2:** Purl across.

Cut yarn and finish off same as Flower 1.

FLOWER BUDS

Wrap your choice of yarn color around your thumb 6-7 times and cut. Tie strand of yarn through lps and another around opposite end, creating tiny lps to look like petal tops. Sew to afghan with tie strands.

FLOWER 3

With Light Blue, wrap yarn around two fingers 20-25 times. Tie in center for pom-pom and trim to make tight. Cut top a little flatter than you would for a regular pom-pom to make it look like a flower. Sew to afghan with tie strands.

FINISHING

Arrange fans, flowers, and leaves on center panel (refer to photo) until you like the effect, then sew each piece on with a whipstitch. Using Light Green and a tapestry needle, work a chain stitch connecting all the flowers and leaves tog. With Dark Lilac and a tapestry needle, work a chain stitch up the RS from bottom point to top point of center motif, in every other st. Rep for left side. Take the two ends at each point and bring them up through to RS of blanket and then back down through to back side to cover the point. Work in all ends.

With Dark Lilac and F-5 hook, join strips by drawing up a lp through first corner at bottom of outer strip and slip stitching through first corner st at bottom of center strip. Sl st back and forth from strip to strip matching rows all the way to the top, finishing on outer strip. End off. Rep for the other side, keeping proper shape when you encounter cables.

Measure out two 90" strands of each color except Light Yellow. Thread all these lengths on a tapestry needle. Leaving a 6" end at the beg, overcast the edge of the afghan with the yarns working through every other sc along the side. Leave a 6" fringe end as you finish. Rep for other side.

Cut 14" lengths of your rem colors, all but Light Yellow. With crochet hook and WS facing, attach 2 strands of each color into every other st along top and bottom. See fringe diagrams on page 118. ❖

Bright Blooms Afghan
Instructions begin on page 70.

Amazing Afghans
FOR COOL KIDS

Your favorite young girls and boys will be the envy of all their friends when you crochet one of these dazzling designs for them. The myriad of colors and unique motifs in these fun and functional creations add a little pizzazz to a child's room.

Show how proud you are of a young athlete by presenting him or her with the "Basketball" afghan after a big game. Take a child on a trip under the sea with "Coral Kingdom," and add a splash of color to a bedroom or playroom with "Far Out!" or "Bright Blooms."

These afghans are sure to be show-stoppers at every show-and-tell, slumber party, and study session. And they may just inspire a new generation of crocheters!

Bright Blooms

These eye-popping blossoms will brighten a young child's room. The rich colors and three-dimensional effect make unique motifs that kids absolutely adore and crocheters love to stitch!

Design by Anita Moore of Calabash, North Carolina

MATERIALS

- **4-ply worsted weight yarn**
  - White (40 oz, 2,080 yds)
  - Yellow (8 oz, 416 yds)
  - Purple (8 oz, 416 yds)
  - Hot Pink (8 oz, 416 yds)
  - Medium Blue (8 oz, 416 yds)
  - Lilac (1 oz, 40 yds)
  - Pale Blue (1 oz, 40 yds)
  - Pink (1 oz, 40 yds)
- **Crochet hooks, size I-9 (5.5 mm) and size J-10 (6.0 mm), or sizes to obtain gauge**
- **Tapestry needle**
- **Sewing needle**
- **3½" piece of cardboard**

DIRECTIONS

FLOWER PETALS
(MAKE 5 PETALS FOR EACH FLOWER)
Note: Make 4 Purple flowers, 4 Pink flowers, and 2 Blue flowers.

With Size I-9 hook, ch 3, join with Sl st in first ch to form a ring. Ch 1.

- **Rnd 1:** 6 sc in ring , join with Sl st to first sc. Ch 1, do not turn.
- **Rnd 2:** 2 sc in each st around, join with Sl st to first sc. Ch 1, do not turn. (12 sc)
- **Rnd 3:** 2 sc in each st around, join with Sl st to first sc. Ch 1, do not turn. (24 sc)
- **Rnd 4:** 1 sc in each st around, join with Sl st to first sc. Ch 1, do not turn. (24 sc)
- **Rnd 5:** (1 sc in first st, 2 sc in next st) rep around, finish off. (36 sc, 3" in diameter)

AFGHAN FINISHED SIZE
Approx 48" × 65"

STITCH GUIDE
Lsc (long single crochet): Insert hook in st indicated, yo, pull up a lp even with lp on hook, yo, draw yarn through both lps on hook.

BLO: Work into only back lp of st.

AFGHAN GAUGE
14 sts = 4" with size J-10 crochet hook

- **Rnd 6:** Join corresponding lighter color with a Sl st in BLO of any st, Sl st in each st around, finish off.

FLOWER CENTERS (MAKE 10)
With Size I-9 hook and Yellow, work Rnds 1-3 of Flower Petal pat, ending work 2 sc in last st, finish off. (25 sc)

Sew 5 petals to each Yellow center using 5 sts on each petal and 5 sts of flower center.

POM-POMS (MAKE 10)
Wrap Yellow yarn 50 times around a 3½" piece of cardboard. Slide yarn off cardboard. Tie center tightly with a double strand of yarn wrapping several times. Cut both ends of pom-pom. Trim to even out balls. Sew 1 pom-pom to each flower center.

AFGHAN
With White and size J-10 hook, ch 166.

- **Row 1:** Sc in second ch from hook, * ch 1, sk next st, sc in next st; rep from * across. Ch 1, turn.
- **Row 2:** Sc in first st, sc in skipped st on Row 1, * sc in next st, sc in skipped st; rep from * across, end sc in last st. Ch 1, turn.
- **Row 3:** Sc in first 2 sts, * ch 1, sk next st, sc in next st; rep from * across, end with an sc in last 2 sts. Ch 1, turn.
- **Row 4:** Sc in first 2 sts, * sc in sk st in Row 2, sc in next st; rep from * across, sc in last st. Ch 1, turn.
- **Row 5:** Sc in first st, * ch 1, sk next st, sc in next st; rep from * across, sc in last st. Ch 1, turn.

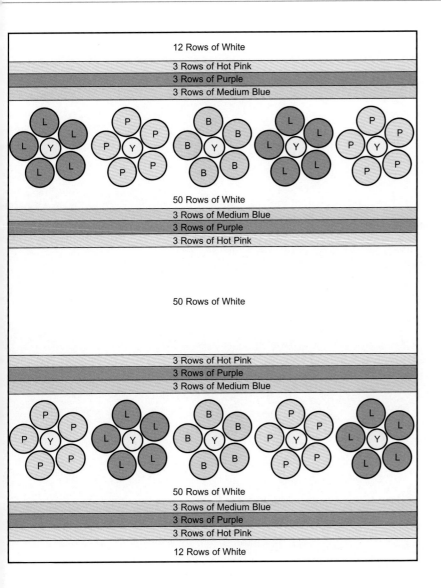

Bright Blooms Key

	White
P	Hot Pink
B	Medium Blue
L	Purple
Y	Yellow

- **Rows 78-79:** Rep Rows 2-3.
- **Rows 80-81:** Drop White, with Medium Blue rep Rows 4-5.
- **Rows 82-85:** Rep Rows 2-5.
- **Rows 86-89:** Drop Medium Blue, with Purple rep Rows 2-5.
- **Rows 90-91:** Rep Rows 2-3.
- **Rows 92-93:** Drop Purple, with Hot Pink rep Rows 4-5.
- **Rows 94-97:** Rep Rows 2-5.
- **Rows 98-145:** Drop Hot Pink, with White rep Rows 2-5 twelve times.

Note: Measure the width of your afghan. It should measure 47½". If the width is more than 47½", change to a smaller size hook. If the width is less then 47½", change to a larger size hook.

- **Rows 6-9:** Rep Rows 2-5.
- **Rows 10-11:** Rep Rows 2-3.
- **Rows 12-13:** Drop White, with Hot Pink rep Rows 4-5.
- **Rows 14-17:** Rep Rows 2-5.
- **Rows 18-21:** Drop Hot Pink, with Purple rep Rows 2-5.
- **Rows 22-23:** Rep Rows 2-3.
- **Rows 24-25:** Drop Purple, with Medium Blue rep Rows 4-5.
- **Rows 26-29:** Rep Rows 2-5.
- **Rows 30-77:** Drop Medium Blue, with White rep Rows 2-5 twelve times.

- **Rows 146-147:** Rep Rows 2-3.
- **Rows 148-233:** Rep Rows 12-97.
- **Rows 234-241:** Drop Hot Pink, with White rep Rows 2-5 twice.
- **Row 242:** Rep Row 2.
- **Row 243 (Border):** Sc in each st across, 3 sc in corner, do not turn, switch to I-9 hook, sc in side of each row across (changing colors where necessary), switch back to size J-10 hook, 3 sc in corner, sc in each st across, 3 sc in corner, switch to size I-9 hook, sc in side of each row across, 2 sc in last st, Sl st to first sc, finish off. Weave in any loose ends.

FINISHING

Sew 5 flowers to each wide White end panel, alternating colors and using chart as a guide. Leave center White panel blank. ❖

Basketball

You'll score big when you stitch this engaging afghan for your favorite young athlete. Crocheting the realistic-looking ball and hoop may just be more fun than the game itself!

Design by Mary Lou Scales of Clinton, Oklahoma

AFGHAN FINISHED SIZE
Approx 48" × 48"

AFGHAN GAUGE
1 square = 6" × 6"
12 dc = 4", 8 rows = 5"
13 sc and 16 rows = 4"

STITCH GUIDE
Lsc (long single crochet): Insert hook in st indicated, yo, pull up a lp even with lp on hook, yo, draw yarn through both lps on hook.

reverse sc: Working from left to right, insert hook in st to the right of hook, yo and draw yarn through, under and to left of lp on hook, yo, and draw yarn through both lps on hook.

BLO: Work into only back lp of st.

picot: Ch 4, Sl st in fourth ch from hook.

MATERIALS

- **4-ply worsted weight yarn**
  - Purple (16 oz, 850 yds)
  - Gold (8 oz, 425 yds)
  - Black (16 oz, 850 yds)
  - Off-White (16 oz, 850 yds)
  - Tan (8 oz, 425 yds)
  - White (3 oz, 160 yds)
  - Red (8 oz, 425 yds)
- **Crochet hook, size I-9 (5.5 mm) or size to obtain gauge**
- **Tapestry needle**
- **Small amount of Fiberfil**

DIRECTIONS

SQUARE A (MAKE 12)
With Black, ch 3, join with a Sl st to form a ring.

- **Rnd 1:** Ch 3, dc in ring, (ch 2, 3 dc) in ring 3 times, ch 2, dc in ring, join with a Sl st to top of ch-3, finish off.

- **Rnd 2:** With Purple yarn, attach with a Sl st to join, ch 3, dc in next dc, * (2 dc, ch 2, 2 dc) in ch-2 sp, dc in next 3 dc; rep from * twice, (2 dc, ch 2, 2 dc) in ch-2 sp, dc in last dc, join with a Sl st to top of ch-3. (4 7-dc groups)

- **Rnd 3:** Ch 3, dc in next 3 dc, * (2 dc, ch 2, 2 dc) in ch-2 sp, dc in next 7 dc; rep from * twice, (2 dc, ch 2, 2 dc) in ch-2 sp, dc in next 3 dc, join with a Sl st to top of ch-3.

- **Rnd 4:** Ch 3, dc in 5 dc, * (2 dc, ch 2, 2 dc) in ch-2 sp, dc in 11 dc; rep from * twice, (2 dc, ch 2, 2 dc) in ch-2 sp, dc in 5 dc, join with a Sl st to top of ch-3, finish off.

- **Rnd 5:** With Black, attach yarn with a Sl st to any st, sc in each st around, 4 sc in each corner, join with a Sl st to first sc, finish off.

SQUARE B (MAKE 12)
Using Gold in place of Purple, rep instructions for square A.

CENTER
With Off-White, ch 92.

- **Row 1:** Dc in fourth ch from hook, dc in each ch across. Ch 3, turn. (90 dc)

- **Row 2:** Dc in each dc across to last dc, work last dc to last 2 lps on hook, yo with Tan yarn and draw yarn through both lps on hook, color change made. Ch 3, turn.

- **Row 3:** Dc in each dc across. Ch 3, turn.

- **Row 4:** Dc in each dc across to last dc, color change to Off-White. Ch 3, turn.

- **Rows 5-7:** Dc in each dc across. Ch 3, turn.

- **Row 8:** Rep Row 2.

- **Rows 9-56:** Rep Rows 3-8 eight times, color change with Tan at end of Row 56.

- **Rows 57 and 58:** Dc in each dc across, color change to Off-White at end of Row 58. Ch 3, turn.

Basketball

- **Rows 59 and 60:** Dc in each dc across, do not finish off at end of Row 60.

BORDER
Ch 1, sc in same st, sc in each dc across, 3 sc in last dc, 90 sc evenly down side, 3 sc in first free lp of beg ch, sc across in each lp, 3 sc in last free lp, 90 sc evenly up side and join with a Sl st to first sc.

BACKBOARD
With Purple, ch 22.

- **Row 1:** Sc in second ch from hook, sc in each ch to last ch; 3 sc in last ch. Working in free lps of beg ch, sc in each free lp across. Ch 1, turn. (43 sc)

- **Row 2 and All Even Rows:** Sc in each sc. Ch 1, turn.

- **Row 3:** Sc in 19 sc, 2 sc in each of 5 sc, sc in 19 sc. Ch 1, turn. (48 sc)

- **Row 5:** Sc in 20 sc, 2 sc in sc, sc in 2 sc, (2 sc in sc, sc in sc) twice, sc in sc, 2 sc in sc, sc in 19 sc. Ch 1, turn. (52 sc)

- **Row 7:** Sc in 21 sc, 2 sc in sc, sc in sc, (2 sc in sc, sc in 2 sc) twice, 2 sc in sc, sc in sc, 2 sc in sc, sc in 20 sc. Ch 1, turn. (57 sc)

- **Row 9:** Sc in 22 sc, 2 sc in sc, sc in 2 sc, (2 sc in sc, sc in 3 sc) twice, 2 sc in sc, sc in 23 sc. Ch 1, turn. (61 sc)

- **Row 11:** Sc in 21 sc, 2 sc in sc, sc in 3 sc, 2 sc in sc, sc in 7 sc, 2 sc in sc, sc in 4 sc, 2 sc in sc, sc in 2 sc, 2 sc in sc, sc in 19 sc. Ch 1, turn. (66 sc)

- **Row 13:** Sc in 23 sc, (2 sc in sc, sc in 3 sc) twice, 2 sc in sc, sc in 4 sc, (2 sc in sc, sc in 3 sc) twice, sc in 22 sc. Ch 1, turn. (71 sc)

- **Row 15:** Sc in 29 sc, 2 sc in sc, sc in 3 sc, 2 sc in sc, sc in 4 sc, 2 sc in sc, sc in 5 sc, 2 sc in sc, sc in 3 sc, 2 sc in sc, sc in 22 sc. Ch 1, turn. (76 sc)

- **Row 17:** Sc in 22 sc, 2 sc in sc, sc in 4 sc, 2 sc in sc, sc in 8 sc, 2 sc in sc, sc in 15 sc, 2 sc in sc, sc in 3 sc, 2 sc in sc, sc in 19 sc. Ch 1, turn. (81 sc)

- **Row 19:** Sc in 25 sc, 2 sc in sc, sc in 4 sc, (2 sc in sc, sc in 7 sc) twice, 2 sc in sc, sc in 5 sc, 2 sc in sc, sc in 28 sc. Ch 1, turn. (86 sc)

- **Row 21:** Sc in 21 sc, 2 sc in sc, sc in 6 sc, 2 sc in sc, sc in 14 sc, 2 sc in sc, sc in 11 sc, 2 sc in sc, sc in 9 sc, 2 sc in sc, sc in 20 sc. Ch 1, turn. (91 sc)

- **Row 23:** Sc in 27 sc, 2 sc in sc, sc in 14 sc, 2 sc in sc, sc in 13 sc, 2 sc in sc, sc in 9 sc, 2 sc in sc, sc in 24 sc. Ch 1, turn. (95 sc)

- **Row 25:** Sc in 25 sc, 2 sc in sc, sc in 10 sc, 2 sc in sc, sc in 11 sc, 2 sc in sc, sc in 12 sc, 2 sc in sc, sc in 14 sc, 2 sc in sc, sc in 18 sc. Ch 1, turn. (100 sc)

- **Row 27:** Sc in 24 sc, 2 sc in sc, sc in 10 sc, (2 sc in sc, sc in 11 sc) twice, 2 sc in sc, sc in 14 sc, 2 sc in sc, sc in 25 sc. Ch 1, turn. (105 sc)

- **Row 29:** Sc in 29 sc, 2 sc in sc, sc in 6 sc, 2 sc in sc, sc in 16 sc, 2 sc in sc, sc in 9 sc, 2 sc in sc, sc in 8 sc, 2 sc in sc, sc in 32 sc. Ch 1, turn. (110 sc)

- **Row 31:** Sc in 24 sc, 2 sc in sc, sc in 13 sc, 2 sc in sc, sc in 14 sc, 2 sc in sc, sc in 17 sc, 2 sc in sc, sc in 12 sc, 2 sc in sc, sc in 25 sc. Ch 1, turn. (115 sc)

- **Row 33:** Sc in each sc. Ch 1, turn.

- **Row 35:** Sc in 24 sc, 2 sc in sc, sc in 14 sc, 2 sc in sc, sc in 17 sc, 2 sc in sc, sc in 8 sc, 2 sc in sc, sc in 6 sc, 2 sc in sc, sc in 41 sc. Ch 1, turn. (120 sc)

- **Row 37:** Sc in 31 sc, 2 sc in sc, sc in 13 sc, 2 sc in sc, sc in 9 sc, 2 sc in sc, sc in 17 sc, 2 sc in sc, sc in 10 sc, 2 sc in sc, sc in 35 sc. Ch 1, turn. (125 sc)

- **Row 39:** Sc in 32 sc, 2 sc in sc, sc in 7 sc, 2 sc in sc, sc in 10 sc, 2 sc in sc, sc in 12 sc, 2 sc in sc, sc in 7 sc, 2 sc in sc, sc in 52 sc. Ch 1, turn. (130 sc)

- **Row 41:** Sc in 23 sc, 2 sc in sc, sc in 13 sc, 2 sc in sc, sc in 18 sc, 2 sc in sc, sc in 20 sc, 2 sc in sc, sc in 15 sc, 2 sc in sc, sc in 36 sc. Ch 1, turn. (135 sc)

- **Row 43:** Sc in 30 sc, 2 sc in sc, sc in 14 sc, 2 sc in sc, sc in 26 sc, 2 sc in sc, sc in 17 sc, 2 sc in sc, sc in 14 sc, 2 sc in sc, sc in 29 sc. Ch 1, turn. (140 sc)

- **Row 45:** Sc in 25 sc, 2 sc in sc, sc in 18 sc, 2 sc in sc, sc in 7 sc, 2 sc in sc, sc in 25 sc, 2 sc in sc, sc in 11 sc, 2 sc in sc, sc in 10 sc, 2 sc in sc, sc in 38 sc. Ch 1, turn. (146 sc)

- **Row 47:** Sc in 40 sc, 2 sc in sc, sc in 8 sc, 2 sc in sc, sc in 25 sc, 2 sc in sc, sc in 34 sc, 2 sc in sc, sc in 5 sc, 2 sc in sc, sc in 29 sc. Ch 1, turn. (151 sc)

- **Row 49:** Sc in 30 sc, 2 sc in sc, sc in 17 sc, 2 sc in sc, sc in 18 sc, (2 sc in sc, sc in 19 sc) twice, 2 sc in sc, sc in 43 sc. (156 sc)

- **Row 50:** Rep Row 2.

BORDER

Attach Gold with a Sl st to BLO of any sc, ch 1, sc in same st, sc in BLO around, 3 sc in corners, join with a Sl st to first sc, finish off.

■ **Rnd 1:** With Black, attach with a Sl st to BLO of center sc in 3-sc corner, ch 1, 3 sc in BLO, sc in BLO of next 30 sc, 2 sc in BLO, sc in 14 BLO, 2 sc in BLO, sc in 16 BLO, 2 sc in BLO, sc in 23 BLO, 2 sc in BLO, sc in 22 BLO, sc in 38 BLO, 3 sc in BLO, sc in each BLO across, join with a Sl st in BLO of first sc.

■ **Rnds 2-4:** Ch 1, sc in BLO of same st, sc in BLO of each sc around and 3 sc in BLO of center sc in 3-sc corner, join with a Sl st to BLO of first sc, finish off after Rnd 4.

BASKETBALL

Note: Basketball is worked in continuous rnds. Do not join unless specified.

With Red, ch 3, join with a Sl st to form ring.

■ **Rnd 1:** Ch 1, 6 sc in ring, place marker, do not join.

■ **Rnd 2:** 2 sc in each sc around. (12 sc)

■ **Rnd 3:** (Sc in sc, 2 sc in sc) around. (18 sc)

■ **Rnd 4:** (Sc in 2 sc, 2 sc in sc) around. (24 sc)

■ **Rnd 5:** (Sc in 3 sc, 2 sc in sc) around. (30 sc)

■ **Rnd 6:** (Sc in 4 sc, 2 sc in sc) around. (36 sc)

■ **Rnd 7:** (Sc in 5 sc, 2 sc in sc) around. (42 sc)

■ **Rnd 8:** (Sc in 6 sc, 2 sc in sc) around. (48 sc)

■ **Rnd 9:** (Sc in 7 sc, 2 sc in sc) around. (54 sc)

■ **Rnd 10:** (Sc in 8 sc, 2 sc in sc) around. (60 sc)

■ **Rnd 11:** Sc in each sc around. (60 sc)

■ **Rnd 12:** (Sc in 5 sc, 2 sc in sc) around. (70 sc)

■ **Rnd 13:** Sc in each sc around. (70 sc)

■ **Rnd 14:** (Sc in 6 sc, 2 sc in sc) around. (80 sc)

■ **Rnd 15:** Sc in each sc around. (80 sc)

■ **Rnd 16:** (Sc in 7 sc, 2 sc in sc) around. (90 sc)

■ **Rnd 17:** Sc in each sc around. (90 sc)

■ **Rnd 18:** (Sc in 8 sc, 2 sc in sc) around. (100 sc)

■ **Rnd 19:** Sc in each sc around. (100 sc)

■ **Rnd 20:** (Sc in 9 sc, 2 sc in sc) around. (110 sc)

■ **Rnd 21:** Sc in each sc around. (110 sc)

■ **Rnd 22:** (Sc in 10 sc, 2 sc in sc) around. (120 sc)

■ **Rnds 23-27:** Sc in each sc around; at end of Rnd 27, join with a Sl st to first sc, finish off.

Using the photo as a guide, embroider a Black chain-stitch to resemble a basketball.

BASKETBALL HOOP

With Black, ch 90, join with a Sl st to form ring. Be careful not to twist ring.

■ **Rnd 1:** Ch 1, sc in each ch around, place marker, join with a Sl st to first sc.

■ **Rnds 2-4:** Sc in each sc around, join with a Sl st at end of each rnd, at end of Rnd 4 finish off.

BASKETBALL NET

■ **Rnd 1:** Attach White to any sc of Rnd 4 with a Sl st, (ch 20, sk 9 sts, sc in next sc) 8 times, ch 10, wrap yarn around hook 5 times, draw lp through same sc as first st of rnd, draw yarn through 2 lps 6 times.

■ **Rnds 2-3:** (Ch 20, sc in ch-20 lp) 8 times, ch 10, wrap yarn around hook 5 times, draw lp through top of last st of prior rnd, draw yarn through 2 lps 5 times.

■ **Rnd 4:** (Ch 20, sc in ch-20 lp) 4 times, (ch 14, using photo as a guide, work picot and attach to central square by drawing a lp through bottom of 35th st from right in fifth row of central square and at same time through fourth ch from hook and through lp on hook, ch 10, sc in ch-20 lp) 5 times having 5 sts bet lps. Fasten off. (9 lps and 4 lps hang free)

JOINING

Using Black, hold blocks RS tog and join by sc in BLO, alternating Block B then Block A to form outside frame. Using Off-White, attach center to frame in same way. Attach backboard to center of afghan from RS with needle and Black yarn. Stuff basketball with Fiberfil and sew basketball on top of backboard using photo as a guide. Sew basketball hoop below basketball centered over top of starting chain of backboard. (front of hoop hangs free)

BORDER

■ **Rnd 1:** Attach Black with a Sl st to BLO of any sc, sc in BLO of each sc, 3 sc in BLO of each corner, join with a Sl st to first sc.

■ **Rnd 2:** Ch 1, sc in each sc around, 3 sc in each corner sc, join with a Sl st to first sc.

■ **Rnd 3:** Ch 1, insert hook into BLO of sc of Rnd 1, Lsc. Lsc in BLO of each sc of Rnd 2 around, work 3 Lsc in BLO of center sc of each corner, join with a Sl st to first sc.

■ **Rnds 4-6:** Rep Rnds 1-3, on Rnd 6 work in sc of Rnd 4.

■ **Rnd 7:** Ch 1, reverse sc in each st around, work 3 reverse sc in each corner st, join with a Sl st to first sc, finish off. ❖

Coral Kingdom
The simple, single crochet stitches make this underwater world come to life right under your fingertips. Just like the real sea, this alluring afghan is full of wonder — and remarkable color!

Design by Norma Gale of Morrison, Colorado

MATERIALS

- **4-ply worsted weight yarn**
  - Light Blue (40 oz, 2,100 yds)
  - Black (24 oz, 1,260 yds)
  - Light Gray (8 oz, 420 yds)
  - Pale Yellow (8 oz, 420 yds)
  - Dark Pink (8 oz, 420 yds)
  - Blue (8 oz, 420 yds)
  - Burgundy (8 oz, 420 yds)
  - White (3 oz, 160 yds)
  - Bright Yellow (3 oz, 160 yds)
  - Red (3 oz, 160 yds)
  - Green (3 oz, 160 yds)
  - Dark Green (3 oz, 160 yds)
  - Medium Purple (3 oz, 160 yds)
  - Orange (3 oz, 160 yds)
  - Dark Orange (3 oz, 160 yds)
  - Bright Orange (3 oz, 160 yds)
  - Dark Red (3 oz, 160 yds)
  - Light Pink (3 oz, 160 yds)

- **4-ply light worsted weight yarn**
  - Lime (5 oz, 290 yds)
  - Hot Pink (5 oz, 290 yds)

- **Crochet hook, size F-5 (3.75 mm) or size to obtain gauge**
- **Tapestry needle**

AFGHAN FINISHED SIZE
Approx 54" × 66"

AFGHAN GAUGE
16 sc and 16 rows = 4"

PATTERN NOTES
- Keeping all loose ends to the WS of your work, pull lp of new color through last 2 lps of previous st. Colors not in use should not be carried across the back more than 3-4 sts. Use a separate ball of yarn for each section of color. You can make bobbins of colors, allowing approx 1 yd for 17 sts.

- When working stripes on the fish, it works better to use a separate bobbin of color for each stripe and each section of color bet stripes. It is easier and looks nicer.

DIRECTIONS

With Black, ch 217.

- **Row 1 (RS):** Sc in second ch from hook and in each ch across, turn. (216 sc)
- **Rows 2-10:** Ch 1, sc in each sc across, turn.
- **Rows 11-65:** Follow chart for panel #1, beg each row with ch 1 and turning at end of each row.
- **Rows 66-74:** With Black, ch 1, sc in each sc across, turn.
- **Rows 75-129:** Follow chart for panel #2, beg each row with ch 1 and turning at end of each row.
- **Rows 130-138:** With Black, ch 1, sc in each sc across, turn.
- **Rows 139-193:** Follow chart for panel #3, beg each row with ch 1 and turning at end of each row.
- **Rows 194-202:** With Black, ch 1, sc in each sc across, turn.
- **Rows 203-257:** Follow chart for panel #4, beg each row with ch 1 and turning at end of each row.

- **Rows 258-265:** With Black, ch 1, sc in each sc across, turn. At end of Row 265, end off.

BORDER

- **Rnd 1:** With RS facing, join Black with sc in first st of top right edge. Working in each st across top and bottom edges and in the end of each row along sides, sc around, working 3 sc in corner sts. Join with Sl st to top of first sc, turn.

- **Rnd 2:** Sl st in each st around, join with Sl st to first Sl st, end off. Fasten and secure all ends. ❖

Coral Kingdom Key

Symbol	Color	Symbol	Color	Symbol	Color
•	White	L	Green	J	Hot Pink
X	Medium Purple	H	Bright Yellow	O	Lime
B	Black	C	Dark Pink	Z	Dark Red
K	Burgundy	N	Red	V	Dark Orange
S	Blue	Y	Light Gray	P	Bright Orange
T	Pale Yellow	E	Orange		
M	Dark Green	A	Light Pink		

Coral Kingdom

Panel 1

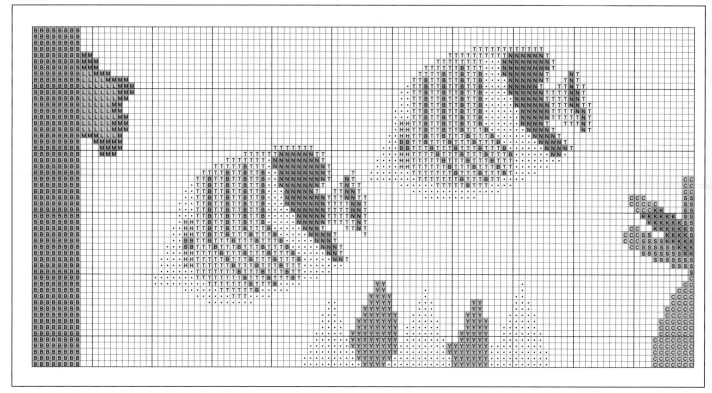

Panel 2

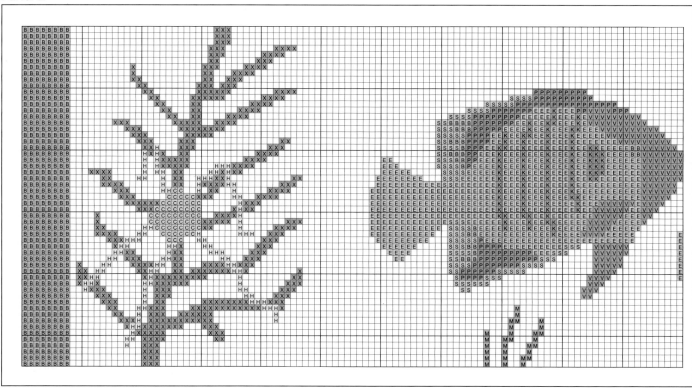

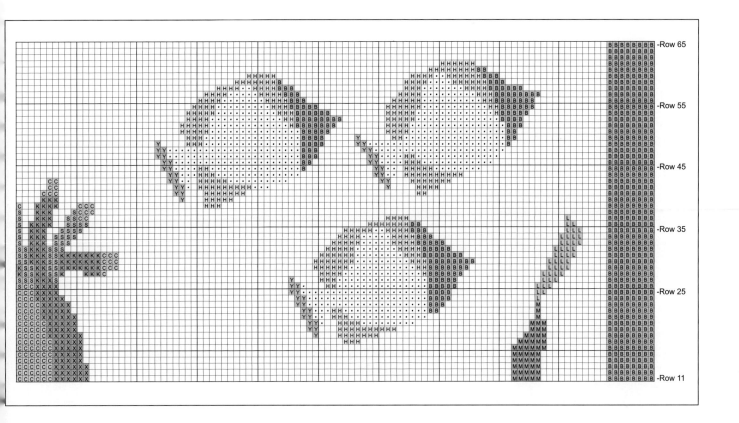

Row 65
Row 55
Row 45
Row 35
Row 25
Row 11

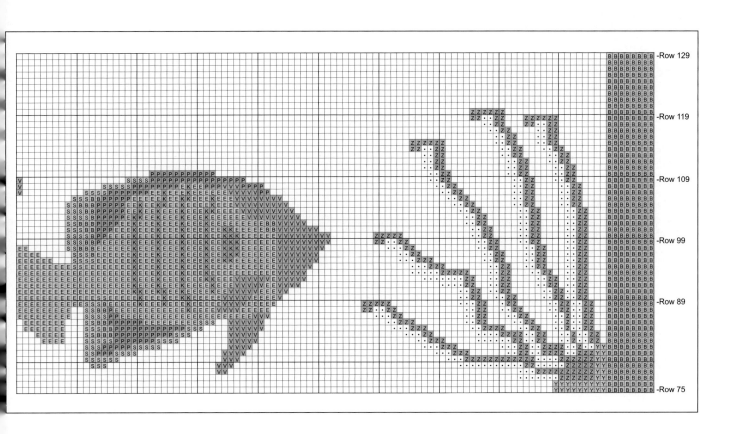

Row 129
Row 119
Row 109
Row 99
Row 89
Row 75

Coral Kingdom

Panel 3

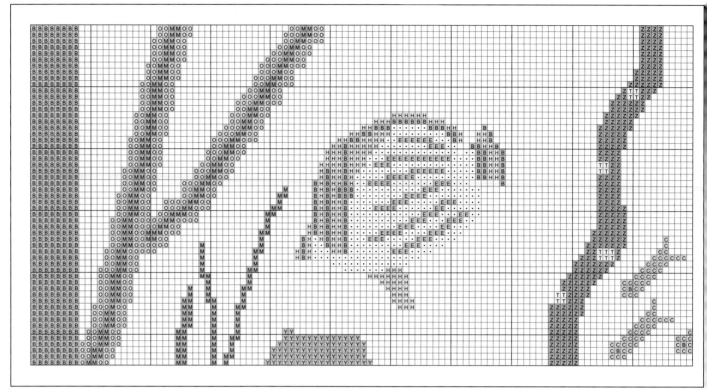

Panel 4

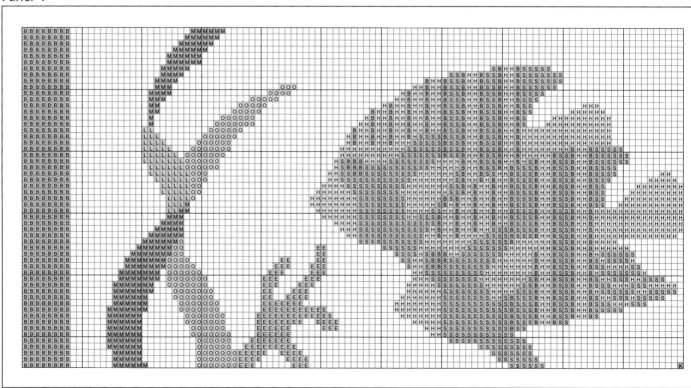

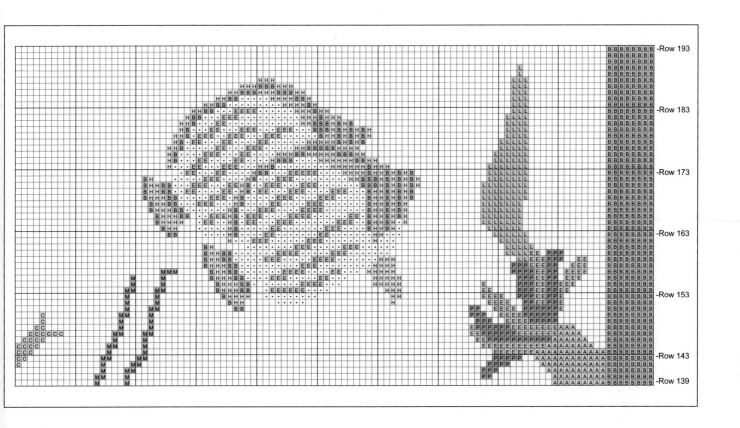

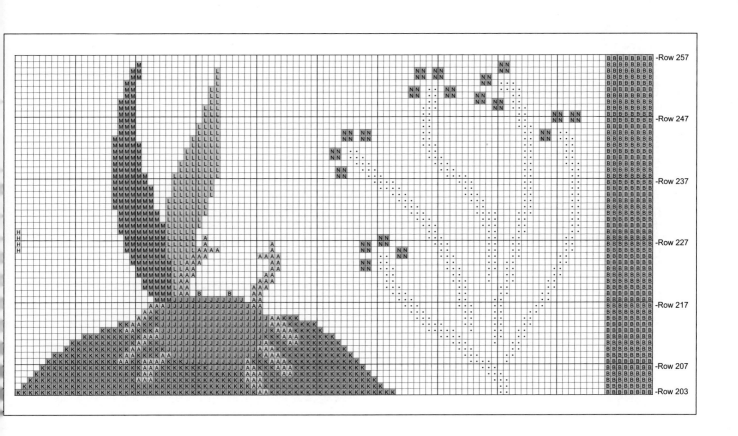

Far Out! Give this groovy blanket to your favorite flower child and she will be the coolest kid on the block! Designed to put a smile on your face and add color to any room, the fun design features nine unique motifs that are out of this world. Neon pony beads and funky fringe add to the afghan's appeal.

Design by Linda Shandy of Billings, Montana

MATERIALS

- **4-ply worsted weight yarn**
  - Bright Multicolor (17½ oz, 945 yds)
  - Hot Pink (12 oz, 640 yds)
  - Lime (12 oz, 640 yds)
  - Light Periwinkle (12 oz, 640 yds)
  - Bright Yellow (12 oz, 640 yds)
- **Crochet hooks, size G-6 (4.0 mm) or size to obtain gauge, and size D-3 (3.25 mm) for pulling lps through bead**
- **1,200 multicolor neon pony beads**

AFGHAN FINISHED SIZE
Approx 49" × 53"

AFGHAN GAUGE
15 sc and 17 rows = 4" × 4"

STITCH GUIDE

ch bd (chain bead): Use smaller crochet hook to draw lp through bead and then draw lp through lp on hook.

sc bd (single crochet bead): Insert hook in next st, draw up a lp, use smaller hook to draw a lp through bead and then draw that lp through 2 lps on hook. (Bead will end up on the WS of work.)

PATTERN NOTES

- Color change: Insert hook into next st, pull up a lp, drop old color behind work, lp new color around hook, draw through both lps on hook. Do not cut yarn until finished with color (counts as 1 sc).
- How to follow graph:
  - Work odd number rows from right to left on graph.
  - Work even rows from left to right on graph.

- When there are large sps bet sections of color, wind a small ball of a color and attach this ball to the start of the new color area.
- Work to within the last st in the color group. With first color, work until there are 2 lps on the hook. Drop the first color, pick up the second color. Yo with the second color and complete the st.

DIRECTIONS

LOVE SQUARE

With Lime, ch 62.

- **Row 1:** Sc in second ch from hook and in each ch across. Ch 1, turn. (61 sc)
- **Rows 2-4:** Sc in each sc across. Ch 1, turn.
- **Row 5:** Sc in 4 sc, color change to Hot Pink, sc in 25 sc, change to Lime, sc in 11 sc, change to Hot Pink, sc 9, change to Lime, sc 12. Ch 1, turn.
- **Rows 6-61:** Follow chart; remember to ch 1, turn at end of each row, and finish off at end of row 61.
- **Outline:** With RS facing, join Bright Multicolor yarn with a Sl st around any post of an sc at the edge of any letter. Ch 1, sc in same st, sc around the posts of

sc on letter edge, join with a Sl st to first sc and finish off. Rep around rem letters.

LOVE BORDER

- **Rnd 1:** With RS facing, join Bright Multicolor yarn with a Sl st to right-most sc of top row, ch 1, 3 sc in same st (corner), sc across to last sc, 3 sc in sc (corner), work 61 sc evenly down side, 3 sc in first free lp of beg ch (corner), sc in each free lp across to last lp, 3 sc in lp (corner), work 61 sc evenly up side, join with a Sl st to first sc. Ch 1, turn.
- **Rnd 2:** Sc in same st, sc in sc, sc bd, (sc in 2 sc, sc bd) 20 times, 3 sc in corner sc, sc bd, (sc in 2 sc, sc bd) 20 times, 3 sc in corner sc, sc in sc, sc bd, (sc in 2 sc,

sc bd) 20 times, 3 sc in (corner) sc, sc in sc, sc bd, (sc in 2 sc, sc bd) 20 times, sc in sc, 3 sc in corner sc, join with a Sl st to first sc. Ch 1, turn.

- **Rnd 3:** Sc in same st, sc in each sc around, 3 sc in center sc of each 3-sc corner, join with a Sl st to first sc, finish off.

DIAMOND SQUARE

With Hot Pink, ch 42.

- **Row 1:** Sc in second ch from hook, sc in 19 more chs, color change to Light Periwinkle, sc in 3 sc, color change to Hot Pink, sc in 19 chs across. Ch 1, turn. (41 sc)

- **Rows 2-61:** Follow chart; remember to ch 1, turn at end of each row, and finish off after row 61.

DIAMOND BORDER

- **Rnd 1:** With RS facing, join Bright Multicolor yarn with a Sl st to right-most sc of top row, ch 1, 3 sc in same st (corner), sc across to last sc, 3 sc in sc (corner), work 61 sc evenly down side, 3 sc in first free lp of beg ch (corner), sc across to last free lp, 3 sc in last lp (corner), work 61 sc evenly down side, join with a Sl st to first sc. Ch 1, turn.

- **Rnd 2:** Sc in same st, (sc in 2 sc, sc bd) 20 times, sc in 2 sc, 3 sc in sc (corner), sc in sc, sc bd, (sc in 2 sc, sc bd) 12 times, sc in 3 sc, 3 sc in sc (corner), sc in sc, sc bd, (sc in 2 sc, sc bd) 20 times, sc in sc, 3 sc in sc (corner), sc in sc, sc bd, (sc in 2 sc, sc bd) 13 times, 3 sc in sc (corner), join with a Sl st to first sc. Ch 1, turn.

- **Rnd 3:** Sc in same st, sc in each sc around, 3 sc in center sc of each 3-sc corner, join with a Sl st to first sc, finish off.

BUTTERFLIES SQUARE

With Hot Pink, ch 52.

- **Row 1:** Sc in second ch from hook and in each ch across. Ch 1, turn. (51 sc)

- **Row 2:** Sc in each sc across. Ch 1, turn.

- **Row 3:** Sc in 30 sc, change to Bright Yellow, sc in 2 sc, change to Hot Pink, sc in 11 sc, change to Bright Yellow, sc in 2 sc, change to Hot Pink, sc in 6 sc.

- **Rows 4-61:** Follow chart; remember to ch 1, turn at end of each row, and finish after row 61.

BUTTERFLIES BORDER

- **Rnd 1:** With RS facing, join Bright Multicolor yarn with a Sl st to right-most sc of top row, ch 1, 3 sc in

same st (corner), sc across to last sc, 3 sc in sc (corner), work 61 sc evenly down side, 3 sc in first free lp of beg ch (corner), sc in each free lp across to last free lp, 3 sc in free lp (corner), work 61 sc evenly up side, join with a Sl st to first sc. Ch 1, turn.

- **Rnd 2:** Sc in same st, (sc in 2 sc, sc bd) 20 times, sc in 2 sc, 3 sc in corner sc, sc in sc, sc bd, (sc in 2 sc, sc bd) 16 times, sc in sc, 3 sc in corner sc, (sc in 2 sc, sc bd) 20 times, sc in 3 sc, 3 sc in corner sc, sc in sc, sc bd, (sc in 2 sc, sc bd) 16 times, sc in sc, 3 sc in corner sc, join with a Sl st to first sc. Ch 1, turn.

- **Rnd 3:** Sc in same st, sc in each sc around, 3 sc in center of each 3-sc corner, join with a Sl st to first sc, finish off.

FLOWERS SQUARE

With Bright Yellow, ch 52.

- **Row 1:** Sc in second ch from hook and in each ch across. Ch 1, turn. (51 sc)

- **Row 2:** Sc in each sc across. Ch 1, turn.

- **Row 3:** Sc in 14 sc, change to Hot Pink, sc in 4 sc, change to Bright Yellow, sc in 33 sc.

- **Rows 4-61:** Follow chart; remember to ch 1, turn at end of each row, and finish off after row 61.

FLOWERS BORDER

- **Rnds 1-3:** Rep instructions for Butterflies Border.

SMILEY SQUARE

With Lime, ch 62.

- **Row 1:** Sc in second ch from hook and in each ch across. Ch 1, turn. (61 sc)

- **Rows 2 and 3:** Sc in each sc across. Ch 1, turn.

- **Row 4:** Sc in 29 sc, color change to Bright Yellow, sc in 3 sc, color change to Lime, sc in 29 sc across.

- **Rows 5-61:** Follow chart; remember to ch 1, turn at end of each row, and finish off after row 61.

- **Outline:** With RS facing, join Bright Multicolor yarn with a Sl st around post of any sc on edge of smiley. Ch 1, sc in same st, sc around posts of all sc on edge of smiley, join with a Sl st to first sc, finish off.

SMILEY BORDER

- **Rnds 1-3:** Rep instructions for Love Border.

WAVE SQUARE

With Bright Yellow, ch 42. Change to Light Periwinkle on last ch. (Be sure to leave a long enough end to secure these two ends.)

- **Row 1:** Sc in second ch from hook, sc in 7 ch, color change to Yellow, sc in 33 ch across. Ch 1, turn. (41 sc)
- **Rows 2-61:** Follow chart; remember to ch 1, turn at end of each row, and finish off after row 61.

WAVE BORDER

- **Rnds 1-3:** Rep instructions for Diamond Border.

SPIRAL SQUARE

With Light Periwinkle, ch 42.

- **Row 1:** Sc in second ch from hook and in each ch across. Ch 1, turn. (41 sc)
- **Row 2:** Sc in each sc across. Ch 1, turn.
- **Row 3:** Sc in 11 sc, color change to Hot Pink, sc in 19 sc, color change to Light Periwinkle, sc in 11 sc across. Ch 1, turn.
- **Rows 4-61:** Follow chart; remember to ch 1, turn at end of each row, and finish off after row 61.

SPIRAL BORDER

- **Rnds 1-3:** Rep instructions for Diamond.

OUTER SPACE SQUARE

With Light Periwinkle, ch 52.

- **Row 1:** Sc in second ch from hook and in each ch across. Ch 1, turn. (51 sc)
- **Row 2:** Sc in each sc across. Ch 1, turn.
- **Row 3:** Sc in 10 sc, color change to Bright Yellow, sc 1, color change to Light Periwinkle, sc in each sc across. Ch 1, turn.
- **Rows 4-61:** Follow chart; remember to ch 1, turn at end of each row, and finish off after row 61.

OUTER SPACE BORDER

- **Rnds 1-3:** Rep instructions for Flowers.

PEACE SQUARE

With Lime, ch 62.

- **Row 1:** Sc in second ch from hook and in each ch across. Ch 1, turn. (61 sc)
- **Rows 2 and 3:** Sc in each sc across. Ch 1, turn.
- **Row 4:** Sc in 3 sc, change to Light Periwinkle, sc 3, change to Green, sc in 9 sc, change to Light Periwinkle, sc 3, change to Lime, sc 8, change to Light Periwinkle, sc 3, change to Lime, sc 2, change to Light Periwinkle, sc 2, change to Lime, sc 5, change to Light Periwinkle, sc 4, change to Lime, sc 9, change to Lime, sc 3, change to Light Periwinkle, sc 7.

Placement Chart

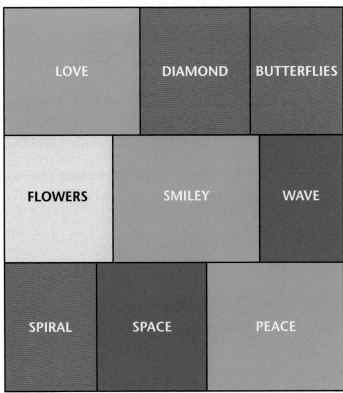

- **Rows 5-61:** Follow chart; remember to ch 1, turn at end of each row, and finish off after row 61.
- **Outline:** With RS facing, join Bright Multicolor yarn with a Sl st to post of any sc on edge of dove, ch 1, sc around same st, sc around posts of all scs around edge of dove, join with a Sl st to first sc, finish off.

PEACE BORDER

- **Rnds 1-3:** Rep instructions for Love.

JOINING

Use placement chart and Bright Multicolor. Holding 2 squares RS facing and beg at corner, join with a Sl st in BLO of both squares. Sl st in each BLO to corner, finish off. Cont until all squares are joined.

FINAL BORDER

- **Rnd 1:** With RS facing and Bright Multicolor, join with a Sl st to any corner, 3 sc in same st, sc in each sc around, 3 sc in each corner sc, join with a Sl st to first sc.
- **Rnd 2:** (Ch 10, ch bd, ch 10, sk sc, Sl st in next sc) rep around entire afghan, join with a Sl st to joining st, finish off.

Note: Due to the beading on this afghan, it is not recommended for use by children under 3 years of age. ❖

Love Square

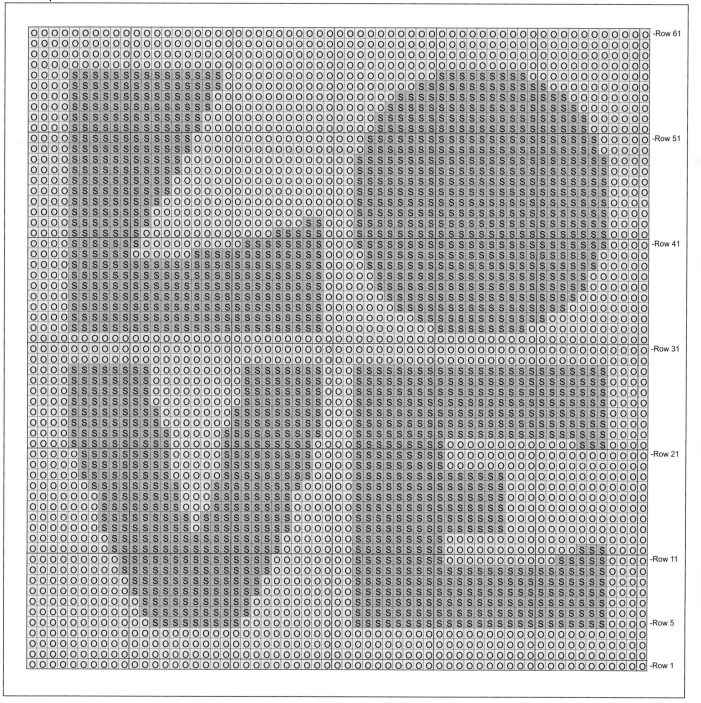

Row 61
Row 51
Row 41
Row 31
Row 21
Row 11
Row 5
Row 1

Love Square Key

S Hot Pink
O Lime

Diamond Square

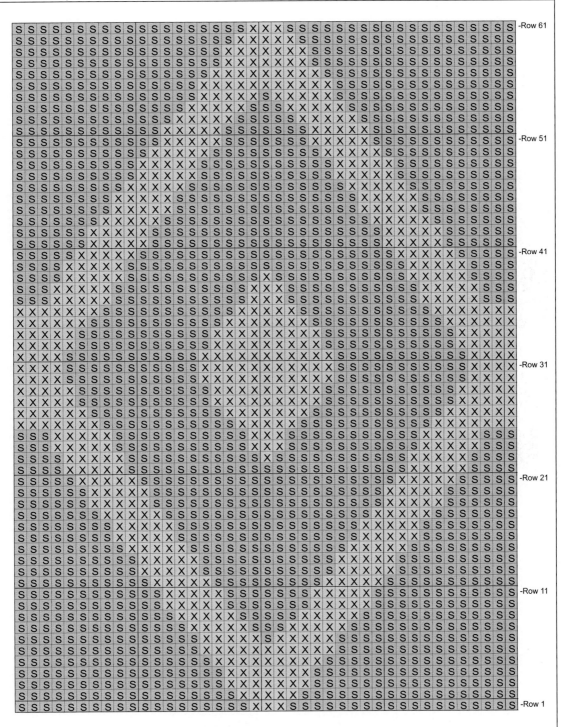

Row 61
Row 51
Row 41
Row 31
Row 21
Row 11
Row 1

Diamond Square Key

S Hot Pink
X Light Periwinkle

Butterflies Square

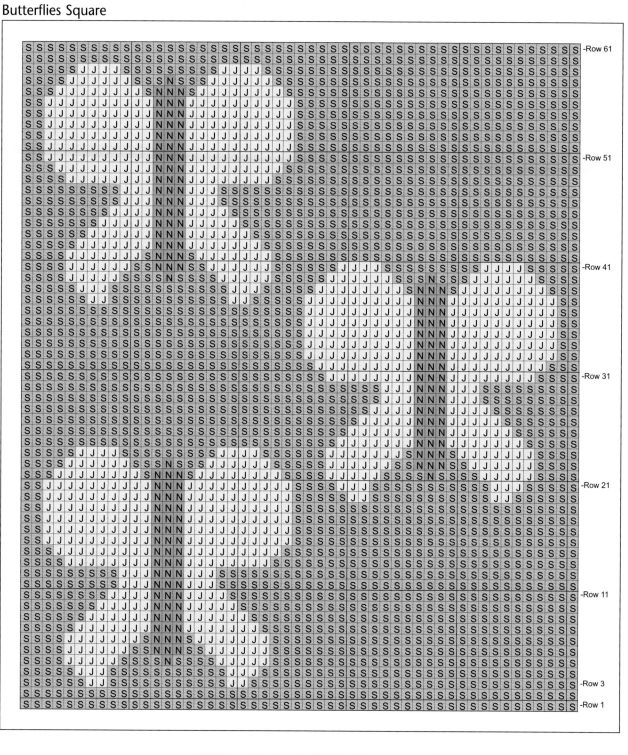

-Row 61
-Row 51
-Row 41
-Row 31
-Row 21
-Row 11
-Row 3
-Row 1

Butterflies Square Key

S Hot Pink

J Bright Yellow

N Bright Multicolor

Flowers Square

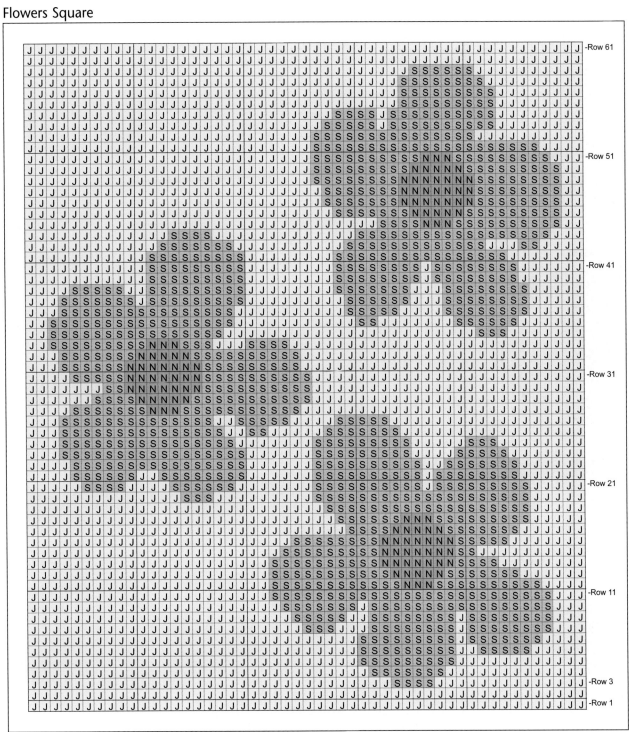

Flowers Square Key

S Hot Pink

J Bright Yellow

N Bright Multicolor

Smiley Square

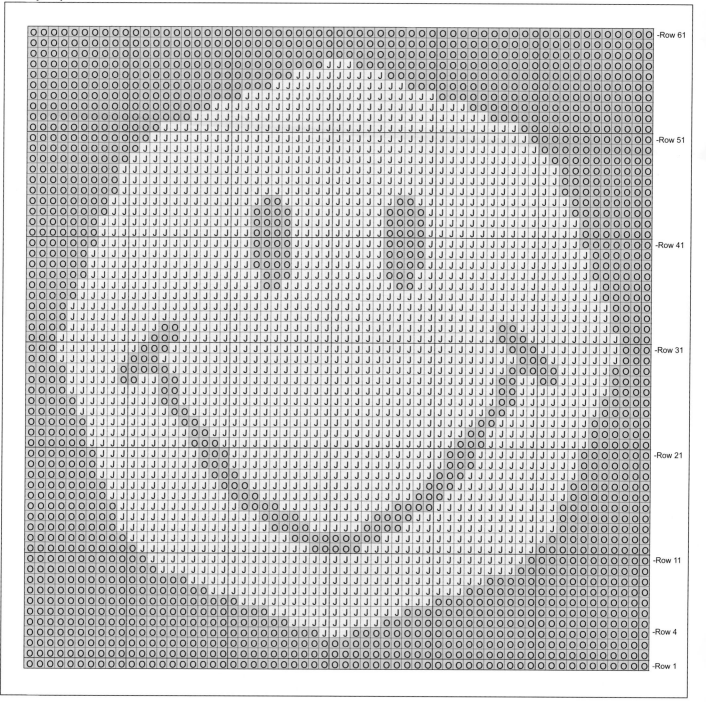

Smiley Square Key

J Bright Yellow

O Lime

Wave Square

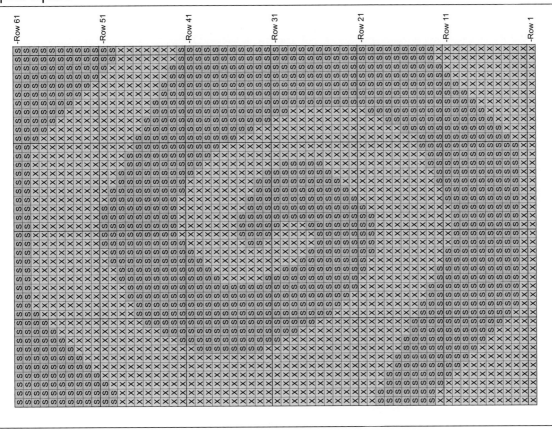

-Row 61 -Row 51 -Row 41 -Row 31 -Row 21 -Row 11 -Row 1

Top

Wave Square Key

| J | Bright Yellow |
| X | Light Periwinkle |

Spiral Square

-Row 61 -Row 51 -Row 41 -Row 31 -Row 21 -Row 11 -Row 1

Top

Spiral Square Key

| S | Hot Pink |
| X | Light Periwinkle |

Outer Space Square

-Row 61
-Row 51
-Row 41
-Row 31
-Row 21
-Row 11
-Row 3
-Row 1

Outer Space Square Key

J Bright Yellow
X Light Periwinkle
N Bright Multicolor

Peace Square

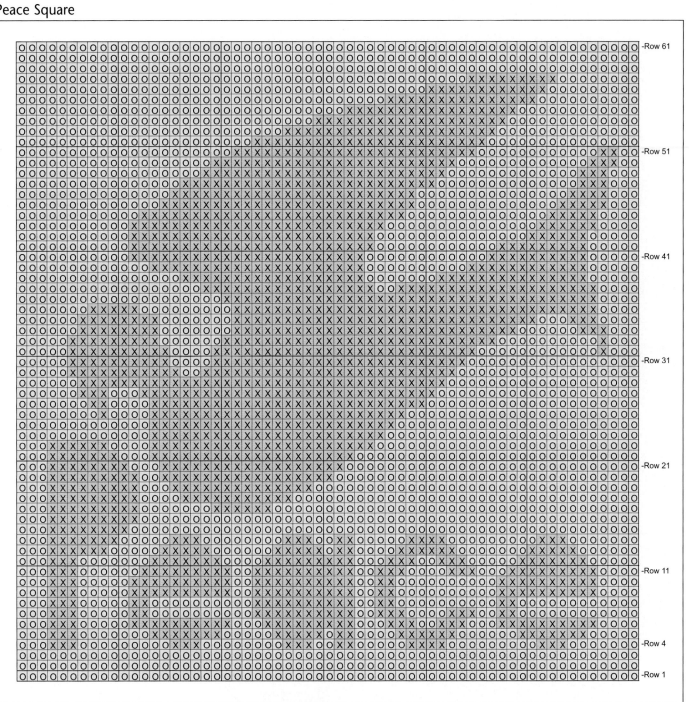

- -Row 61
- -Row 51
- -Row 41
- -Row 31
- -Row 21
- -Row 11
- -Row 4
- -Row 1

Peace Square Key

X   Light Periwinkle

O   Lime

Desert Warmth Afghan
Instructions begin on page 96.

Embroidered Afghans
FOR WARMTH & STYLE

Combining crocheting and cross-stitch results in breathtaking designs that are a pleasure to create and a joy to use. Worked first in the afghan stitch (also called the Tunisian stitch), the gorgeous motifs on the following four afghans are then cross-stitched over the top. Thick and cozy, and equally striking, the comfy coverlets are extraordinary home accents and excellent lap warmers.

The appealing afghans offer varied delights to charm every taste. Stitch a Southwest scene with the "High Plains" afghan or a sunflower sensation with "Trip Around the Sunflower." Add country charm to your sitting room with the lovely "Tunisian Hearts" throw or give your home a bit of Native American flavor with "Desert Warmth."

Made as gifts for your family and friends or stitched for your own home, these embroidered afghans will hold heartfelt memories for years to come.

Desert Warmth

Bright colors of red and orange are toned and warmed with shades of brown and pale yellow—reminiscent of Native American blankets, but with a dramatic, modern look! You'll enjoy embroidering the motifs and then dreaming of the desert's warmth as you snuggle in with it on a chilly day.

Design by Donna Leister of Salem, Indiana

MATERIALS

- **4-ply worsted weight yarn**
  - Red (40 oz, 2,100 yds)
  - Black (8 oz, 420 yds)
  - Pale Yellow (8 oz, 420 yds)
  - Orange (6 oz, 320 yds)
  - Brown (3 oz, 160 yds)
- **22" afghan hook, size G-6 (4.0 mm) or size to obtain gauge**
- **Crochet hook, size G-6 (4.0 mm) or size to obtain gauge**
- **Tapestry needle**

Desert Warmth Key

CROSS-STITCH

☐	Red
B	Black
V	Pale Yellow
O	Orange
X	Brown

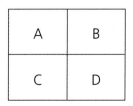

AFGHAN FINISHED SIZE
Approx 43" × 53"

AFGHAN GAUGE
16 sts = 4" in afghan stitch

STITCH GUIDE

afghan stitch: This stitch is completed in two halves (referred to as one row in instructions). In the first half, leave all lps on hook; in the second half, work lps off. Do not turn work throughout. Use an afghan hook.

1) **Make a ch of instructed length.**
   Note: On ch row only, insert hook through one top lp instead of both.

2) **Row 1A (first half):** Insert hook into top lp of second ch from hook, yo, draw up a lp. Rep in each ch across (Fig. 1A). Leave all lps on hook.

3) **Row 1B (second half):** Work off lps. Yo, draw through first lp on hook, * yo and draw through 2 lps; rep from * across (Fig. 1B). The last lp remaining on hook always counts as first st of next row.

4) **Row 2A (first half):** Keeping all lps on hook, insert hook behind second vertical bar (Fig. 2A), yo and draw through a lp. Rep for each bar across, ending insert hook under last bar and the st directly behind it, yo and draw up a lp (Fig. 2B). This makes a firm edge.

5) **Row 2B (second half):** Rep Row 1B.

6) **Rep Row 2 (A and B) for pattern.** To finish, Sl st in each bar across.

cross-stitch over afghan stitch: Cross-stitch over afghan stitch is worked from a chart with a key for the symbols and colors used. Each square on chart represents one bar. One cross-stitch is worked over one vertical bar. To work cross-stitch, count over required number of bars to where you wish to begin. Bring yarn through from back of work to front, leaving 2" end to be worked over (do not knot). Work cross-stitches as shown in Fig. 3, being careful not to pull stitches too tightly. Be sure that all the top legs of the cross-stitches lie in the same direction. When finished with a strand of yarn, do not knot, weave in end through sts on back of afghan.

Afghan Stitch
FIG. 1A

FIG. 1B

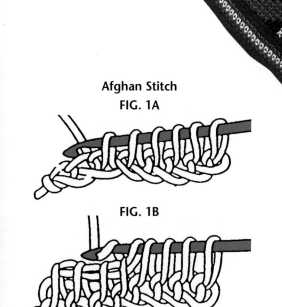

FIG. 2A

FIG. 2B

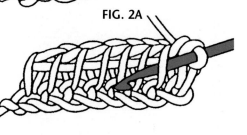

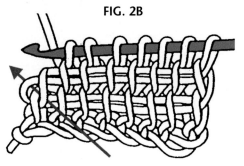

Cross-Stitch Over Afghan Stitch
FIG. 3

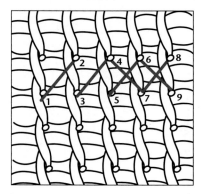

DIRECTIONS

With afghan hook and Red, ch 161. Work in afghan stitch for 200 rows. End off.

BORDER

■ **Rnd 1:** With Sl st of Red on crochet hook, attach in any corner. Ch 1, 3 sc in corner; work sc along each edge (1 sc in each row across side, sc in each st across top and bottom), and 3 sc in each corner around. Join with Sl st to first sc.

■ **Rnd 2:** Sl st to corner sc, ch 1, 3 sc in corner, sc in each sc around and 3 sc in each corner. End off Red.

■ **Rnd 3:** With Sl st of Orange on hook, join to any corner. 3 sc in corner, sc in each sc around, ch 1, 3 sc in each corner. End off Orange.

■ **Rnd 4:** With Pale Yellow, rep Rnd 3.

■ **Rnd 5:** With Orange, rep Rnd 3.

■ **Rnds 6-7:** With Red, rep Rnd 3. End off, fasten and secure all ends.

EMBROIDERY

Work stitches as shown on the chart. Do not carry yarn across more than 3-4 stitches on the back. ❖

Desert Warmth

See key and diagram on page 96.

See key and diagram on page 96.

Desert Warmth

ⓒ

See key and diagram on page 96.

Desert Warmth

See key and diagram on page 96.

High Plains

A warm picture of the beautiful American Southwest emerges as you stitch this fabulous afghan. Crocheting this breathtaking scene is like painting with yarn, and when it is complete you'll have a handmade masterpiece!

Design by Frieda Harris of Alamogordo, New Mexico

MATERIALS

- 4-ply worsted weight yarn
  - Burgundy (35 oz, 1,820 yds)
  - Light Brown (35 oz, 1,820 yds)
  - Very Dark Brown (14 oz, 728 yds)
  - Lavender (2 oz, 104 yds)
  - Light Lavender (2 oz, 104 yds)
  - Light Gold (1 oz, 52 yds)
  - Gold (2 oz, 104 yds)
  - Dark Lavender (3 oz, 156 yds)
  - Dark Coral (4 oz, 208 yds)
  - Coral (3 oz, 156 oz)
  - Very Light Pink (1 oz, 52 yds)
  - Medium Brown (1 oz, 52 yds)
  - Dark Blue Green (1 oz, 52 yds)
  - Dark Tan (2 oz, 104 yds)
  - Cream (4 oz, 208 yds)
  - Dark Orange Brown (1 oz, 52 yds)
  - Dark Orange Tan (2 oz, 104 yds)
  - Orange Tan (2 oz, 104 yds)
  - Brown Black (4 oz, 208 yds)
  - Dark Brown (2 oz, 104 yds)
  - Pink (1 oz, 52 yds)
  - Blue Green (2 oz, 105 yds)
  - Dark Green (1 oz, 52 yds)
- Afghan hook, size H-8 (5.0 mm) or size to obtain gauge
- Crochet hook, size H-8 (5.0 mm) or size to obtain gauge
- Tapestry needle

AFGHAN FINISHED SIZE
Approx 60" × 60"
H-8 afghan hook

AFGHAN GAUGE
16 sts = 4" in afghan stitch with size
16 sts = 4" in border pattern

STITCH GUIDE
Note: Refer to stitch diagrams on page 97 for afghan stitch and cross-stitch over afghan stitch.

afghan stitch: This stitch is completed in two halves (referred to as one row in instructions). In the first half, leave all lps on hook; in the second half, work lps off. Do not turn work throughout. Use an afghan hook.

1) **Make a ch of instructed length.**
   Note: On ch row only, insert hook through one top lp instead of both.

2) **Row 1A (first half):** Insert hook into top lp of second ch from hook, yo, draw up a lp. Rep in each ch across (Fig. 1A). Leave all lps on hook.

3) **Row 1B (second half):** Work off lps. Yo, draw through first lp on hook, * yo and draw through 2 lps; rep from * across (Fig. 1B). The last lp remaining on hook always counts as first st of next row.

4) **Row 2A (first half):** Keeping all lps on hook, insert hook behind second vertical bar (Fig. 2A), yo and draw through a lp. Rep for each bar across, ending insert hook under last bar and the st directly behind it, yo and draw up a lp (Fig. 2B). This makes a firm edge.

5) **Row 2B (second half):** Rep Row 1B.

6) **Rep Row 2 (A and B) for pattern.** To finish, Sl st in each bar across.

cross-stitch over afghan stitch: Cross-stitch over afghan stitch is worked from a chart with a key for the symbols and colors used. Each square on chart represents one bar. One cross-stitch is worked over one vertical bar. To work cross-stitch, count over required number of bars to where you wish to begin. Bring yarn through from back of work to front, leaving 2" end to be worked over (do not knot). Work cross-stitches as shown in Fig. 3, being careful not to pull stitches too tightly. Be sure that all the top legs of the cross-stitches lie in the same direction. When finished with a strand of yarn, do not knot, weave in end through sts on back of afghan.

FPdc (front post double crochet): Yo, insert hook from front around the post of next st, coming out again at the front or other side of post, yo, draw up a lp, (yo, draw though 2 lps) twice. (Fig. 4)

shell: 5 dc in designated stitch.

FIG. 4

TIP

This afghan is great for using up scraps of yarn, as a variety of colors are used to create the cross-stitched image. Use the chart and photo as a guide, but experiment with different shades of yarn using what you have on hand to cross-stitch the Southwest scene!

DIRECTIONS

With size H-8 afghan hook and Burgundy yarn, ch 168.

CENTER

Work in afghan stitch for 149 rows. Fasten off.

EMBROIDERY

Beg in the lower right corner of the afghan center, count up one row and one st over. Following the chart, use a tapestry needle to work all the cross-stitches with one strand of yarn on the RS of the afghan center. *Note: You should have one Burgundy st at the beg and end of each row, and one row of Burgundy sts on the top and bottom. This Burgundy "border" around the embroidered design is shown as a border of blank sts on the cross-stitch chart. Use one strand of yarn to work all backstitches.*

BORDER

Note: When working dcs in the top row of the afghan stitch, yo, insert hook behind next vertical bar and into sp just to the left of this stitch (hook will be pointing to the back). Yo, draw up lp, (yo, draw through 2 lps) twice. This prevents holes in the top row of the afghan. With size H-8 crochet hook and Light Brown, join with Sl st in upper right corner of afghan.

High Plains

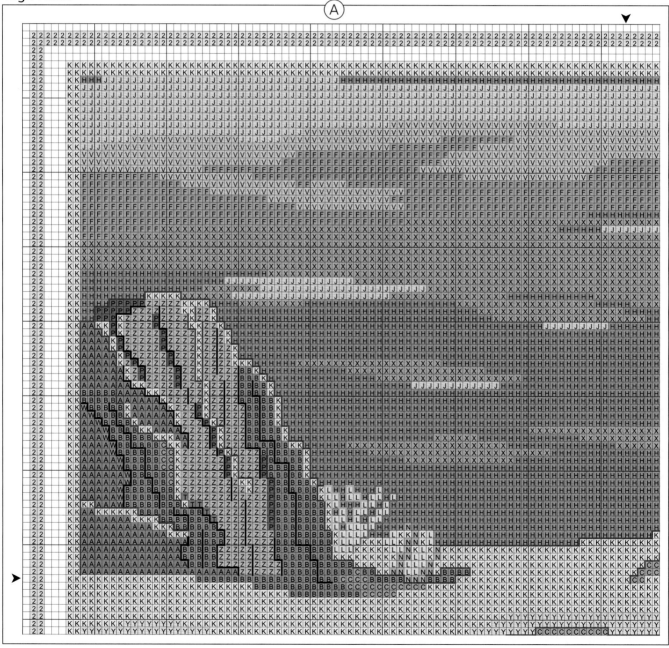

High Plains Key

CROSS-STITCH

X	Lavender
J	Light Lavender
Y	Light Gold
2	Gold
H	Dark Lavender
S	Dark Coral
U	Coral
V	Very Light Pink
W	Medium Brown

CROSS-STITCH

G	Dark Blue Green
Z	Dark Tan
K	Cream
A	Dark Orange Brown
C	Dark Orange Tan
B	Orange Tan
T	Brown Black
P	Dark Brown
F	Pink

CROSS-STITCH

L	Blue Green
N	Dark Green

BACKSTITCH

— Green
— Very Dark Brown
— Brown Black
— Dark Green

STEM STITCH

— Brown Black

Stem Stitch

A	B
C	D

High Plains

- **Rnd 1:** Ch 3, (dc, ch 2, 2 dc) in same corner st, dc in each st across top, (2 dc, ch 2, 2 dc) in last st, dc in each row going down side, (2 dc, ch 2, 2 dc) in first st of bottom of afghan, dc in each st across, (2 dc, ch 2, 2 dc) in last st, dc in each row going up side. Join with Sl st in top of beg ch-3. (top and bottom = 165 dc each, plus corners; sides = 147 dc each, plus corners)

- **Rnd 2:** Sl st in next st and ch-2 sp, (ch 3, dc, ch 2, 2 dc) in corner ch-2 sp, * sk next dc, (2 FPdc, 2 dc) across to last 4 dc before corner; 2 FPdc, 1 dc, sk last dc, (2 dc, ch 2, 2 dc) in next corner sp, sk next dc, (2 Fpdc, 2 dc) across to last st before corner, sk last dc **, (2 dc, ch 2, 2 dc); rep from * around, ending at ** on the last side. Join with Sl st in top of beg ch-3. (top and bottom = 167 dc each, plus corners; sides = 149 dc each, plus corners)

- **Rnd 3:** Sl st in next st and ch-2 sp, (ch 3, dc, ch 2, 2 dc) in corner ch-2 sp, * (2 dc, 2 FPdc) across to last 3 dc before corner, 2 dc, FPdc, (2 dc, ch 2, 2 dc) in next corner sp, (2 dc, 2 FPdc) across to last 3 dc before corner, 2 FPdc, 1 dc **, (2 dc, ch 2 2 dc) in next corner sp; rep from * around, ending at ** on the last side. Join with Sl st in top of beg ch-3. (top and bottom = 173 dc each, plus corners; sides = 153 dc each, plus corners)

- **Rnd 4:** Sl st in next st and ch-2 sp, (ch 3, dc, ch 2, 2 dc) in corner ch-2 sp, * sk next dc, dc in next dc, (2 FPdc, 2 dc) across to last 3 dc before corner, 2 dc, sk last dc **, (2 dc, ch 2, 2 dc) in next corner sp; rep from * around, ending at ** on the last side. Join with Sl st in top of beg ch-3. (top and bottom = 173 dc each, plus corners; sides = 155 dc, plus corners)

- **Rnd 5:** Sl st in next st and ch-2 sp, (ch 3, dc, ch 2, 2 dc) in corner ch-2 sp, * sk next dc, dc in next 2 dc, (2 FPdc, 2 dc) across to last 4 dc, 2 FPdc, dc, sk last dc (2 dc, ch 2, 2 dc) in next corner sp, sk next dc, dc in next 2 dc, (2 FPdc, 2 dc) across to last 2 dc, FPdc, sk last dc **, (2 dc, ch 2, 2 dc) in next corner sp; rep from * around, ending at ** on the last side. Join

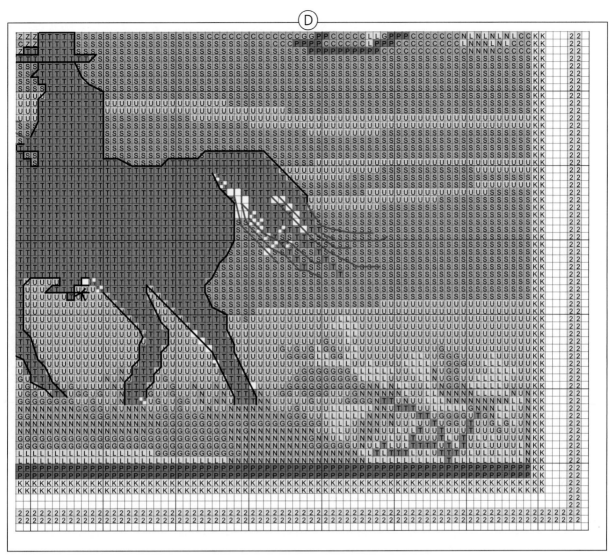

with Sl st in top of beg ch-3. (top and bottom = 175 dc each, plus corners; sides = 157 dc each, plus corners)

- **Rnds 6-8:** Rep Rnds 3-5.

- **Rnds 9-10:** Rep Rnds 3-4 again. (top and bottom = 193 dc, including corners; sides = 175 dc each, including corners at end of Rnd 10)

- **Rnd 11 (Shell Rnd):** Sl st in next st and ch-2 sp, * 7 dc in same corner ch-2 sp, sk 1, sc in next st, (sk 2, 5 dc in next st, sk 2, sc in next st) 15 times, (sk 1, 5 dc in next st, sk 1, sc in next st) twice, (sk 2, 5 dc in next st, sk 2, sc in next st) 15 times, sk 1, sc in next st, sk 1; 7 dc in next corner, sk 1, sc in next st, (sk 2, 5 dc in next st, sk 2, sc in next st) 14 times, sk 2; rep from * around. Join with Sl st in top of first st.

- **Rnd 12:** Sc in each st around, working 3 sc in each corner st. Fasten off.

- **Rnds 13-14:** Join Very Dark Brown in corner with Sl st, ch 1; rep Rnd 12.

- **Rnd 15 (Shell Rnd):** Sl st to corner st, * 7 dc in corner st, sk 1, sc in next st, (sk 2, 5 dc in next st, sk 1, sc in next st) 27 times, (sk 1, 5 dc in next st, sk 1, sc in next st) once, (sk 2, 5 dc in next st, sk 2, sc in next st) 27 times, sk 1, sc in next st, sk 1, 7 dc in next corner, sk 1, sc in next st, (sk 2, 5 dc in next st, sk 2, sc in next st) 24 times, (sk 1, 5 dc in next st, sk 1, sc in next st) once, (sk 2, 5 dc in next st, sk 2, sc in next st) 25 times, sk 1, sc in next st; rep from * around. Join with Sl st in top of first st.

- **Rnd 16:** Rep Rnd 12. Fasten off.

- **Rnd 17:** Join Light Brown with Sl st in any corner st. Rep Shell Rnd in Rnd 15, spacing as necessary.

- **Rnd 18:** Rep Rnd 12.

- **Rnd 19:** Hdc in each st around, working 3 hdc in each corner st.

- **Rnds 20-22:** Rep Rnd 12. Fasten off at the end of Rnd 22.

- **Rnd 23-25:** Join Very Dark Brown in any corner st with Sl st. Rep Rnd 12. Fasten off at the end of Rnd 25. ❖

Trip Around the Sunflower

Sunflowers galore adorn this bright and bold blanket. A great take-along project, each embroidered square is filled with fun and color. This is the ideal afghan for that special flora-filled sunroom.

Design by D. Michelle Jones-Lewis of Victorville, California

MATERIALS

- **4-ply worsted weight yarn**
  - White (72 oz, 3,780 yds)
  - Green (6 oz, 320 yds)
  - Blue (6 oz, 320 yds)
  - Dark Green (6 oz, 320 yds)
  - Red (3 oz, 160 yds)
  - Black (3 oz, 160 yds)
  - Orange (3 oz, 160 yds)
  - Brown (3 oz, 160 yds)
  - Purple (3 oz, 160 yds)
  - Light Blue (7 oz, 396 yds)
  - Gold (7 oz, 396 yds)
  - Dark Brown (7 oz, 396 yds)
  - Light Yellow (3½ oz, 198 yds)
- **Afghan hook, size H-8 (5.0 mm) or size to obtain gauge**
- **Crochet hook, size F-5 (3.75 mm) or size to obtain gauge**
- **Tapestry needle**

AFGHAN FINISHED SIZE
Approx 55" × 66", not including fringe

AFGHAN GAUGE
15 sts = 4" in afghan stitch with H-8 afghan hook

STITCH GUIDE
Note: Refer to stitch diagrams on page 97 for afghan stitch and cross-stitch over afghan stitch.

afghan stitch: This stitch is completed in two halves (referred to as one row in instructions). In the first half, leave all lps on hook; in the second half, work lps off. Do not turn work throughout. Use an afghan hook.

1) **Make a ch of instructed length.**
   Note: On ch row only, insert hook through one top lp instead of both.

2) **Row 1A (first half):** Insert hook into top lp of second ch from hook, yo, draw up a lp. Rep in each ch across (Fig. 1A). Leave all lps on hook.

3) **Row 1B (second half):** Work off lps. Yo, draw through first lp on hook, * yo and draw through 2 lps; rep from * across (Fig. 1B). The last lp remaining on hook always counts as first st of next row.

4) **Row 2A (first half):** Keeping all lps on hook, insert hook behind second vertical bar (Fig. 2A), yo and draw through a lp. Rep for each bar across, ending insert hook under last bar and the st directly behind it, yo and draw up a lp (Fig. 2B). This makes a firm edge.

5) **Row 2B (second half):** Rep Row 1B.

6) **Rep Row 2 (A and B) for pattern.** To finish, Sl st in each bar across.

cross-stitch over afghan stitch: Cross-stitch over afghan stitch is worked from a chart with a key for the symbols and colors used. Each square on chart represents one bar. One cross-stitch is worked over one vertical bar. To work cross-stitch, count over required number of bars to where you wish to begin. Bring yarn through from back of work to front, leaving 2" end to be worked over (do not knot). Work cross-stitches as shown in Fig. 3, being careful not to pull stitches too tightly. Be sure that all the top legs of the cross-stitches lie in the same direction. When finished with a strand of yarn, do not knot, weave in end through sts on back of afghan.

Trip Around the Sunflower

DIRECTIONS

BACKGROUND SQUARES (MAKE 25)

With White yarn and H-8 afghan hook, ch 41.

■ **Rows 1-45:** Work in afghan stitch. Do not end off, but change to F-5 crochet hook and work one rnd of sc around the square, working in each st and row, with 3 sc in each corner. End off, fasten and secure ends.

EMBROIDERY

Follow the cross-stitch charts to make the sunflower designs, as follows:

■ California Sunflower: Make 5.

■ German Bliss Sunflower: Make 8.

■ Mexican Sunflower: Make 4.

■ Nebraska Sunflower: Make 8.

Work all backstitching with Black yarn.

When your cross-stitching is done, whipstitch all squares tog following the placement chart.

BORDER

With Dark Green and F-5 crochet hook, join with Sl st in any corner, sc in same st, (ch 12, sc in next st) around, ending by joining with Sl st to the first sc. ❖

California Sunflower

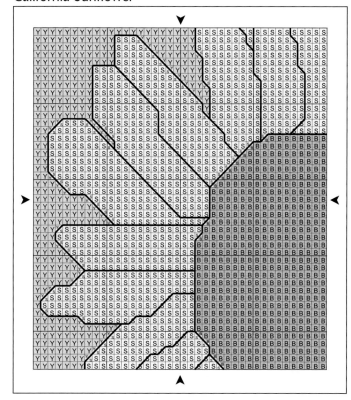

German Bliss Sunflower

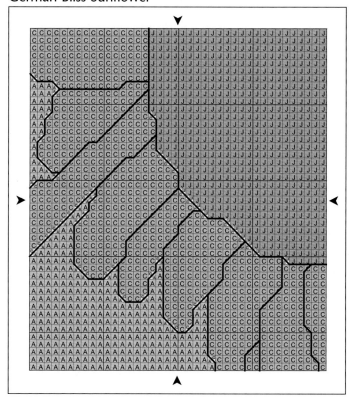

California Sunflower Key

CROSS-STITCH		BACKSTITCH	
B	Brown	—	Black
S	Light Yellow		
Y	Light Blue		

German Bliss Sunflower Key

CROSS-STITCH		BACKSTITCH	
C	Red	—	Black
A	Purple		
J	Dark Brown		

Placement Chart

C	N	G	N	C
N	G	M	G	N
G	M	C	M	G
N	G	M	G	N
C	N	G	N	C

C California Sunflower

G German Bliss Sunflower

M Mexican Sunflower

N Nebraska Sunflower

Mexican Sunflower

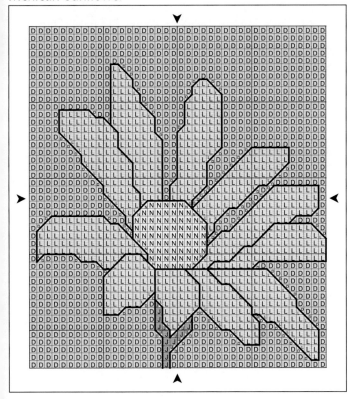

Nebraska Sunflower

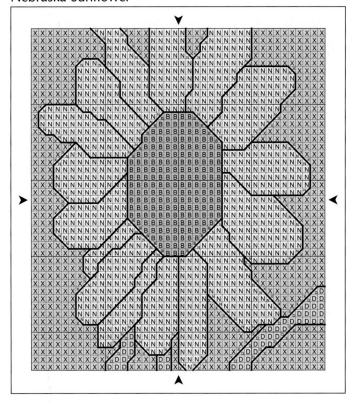

Mexican Sunflower Key

CROSS-STITCH   BACKSTITCH

N Gold   — Black

L Orange

J Dark Brown

D Dark Green

Nebraska Sunflower Key

CROSS-STITCH   BACKSTITCH

B Brown   — Black

N Gold

D Dark Green

X Blue

Tunisian Hearts

Whether you love Tunisian crochet or cross-stitch embroidery, this beautifully detailed design will be a joy to create. You'll be drawn to the country colors and simple motifs that make the afghan a wonderful accent for a bedroom or porch.

Design by Elizabeth Anne Riley of Columbus, Ohio

MATERIALS

- **4-ply worsted weight yarn**
  - Soft White (64 oz, 3,400 yds):
    Color A (CA)
  - Country Blue (16 oz, 850 yds):
    Color B (CB)
  - Light Green (6 oz, 326 yds)
  - Dark Pink (3 oz, 163 yds)
  - Dark Red (3 oz, 163 yds)
- **Afghan hook, size J-10 (6.0 mm) or size to obtain gauge**
- **Crochet hook, size F-5 (3.75 mm) or size to obtain gauge**
- **Tapestry needle**

AFGHAN FINISHED SIZE
Approx 55" × 59½"

AFGHAN GAUGE
15 sts and 14 rows = 4"

STITCH GUIDE

Note: Refer to stitch diagrams on page 97 for afghan (Tunisian simple) stitch and cross-stitch over afghan stitch.

Tss (Tunisian simple stitch/afghan stitch): This stitch is completed in two halves (referred to as one row in instructions). In the first half, leave all lps on hook; in the second half, work lps off. Do not turn work throughout. Use an afghan hook.

1) **Make a ch of instructed length.** *Note: On ch row only, insert hook through one top lp instead of both.*

2) **Row 1A (first half):** Insert hook into top lp of second ch from hook, yo, draw up a lp. Rep in each ch across (Fig. 1A). Leave all lps on hook.

3) **Row 1B (second half):** Work off lps. Yo, draw through first lp on hook, * yo and draw through 2 lps; rep from * across (Fig. 1B). The last lp remaining on hook always counts as first st of next row.

4) **Row 2A (first half):** Keeping all lps on hook, insert hook behind second vertical bar (Fig. 2A), yo and draw through a lp. Rep for each bar across, ending insert hook under last bar and the st directly behind it, yo and draw up a lp (Fig. 2B). This makes a firm edge.

5) **Row 2B (second half):** Rep Row 1B.

6) **Rep Row 2 (A and B) for pattern.** To finish, Sl st in each bar across.

cross-stitch over afghan stitch: Cross-stitch over afghan stitch is worked from a chart with a key for the symbols and colors used. Each square on chart represents one bar. One cross-stitch is worked over one vertical bar. To work cross-stitch, count over required number of bars to where you wish to begin. Bring yarn through from back of work to front, leaving 2" end to be worked over (do not knot). Work cross-stitches as shown in Fig. 3, being careful not to pull stitches too tightly. Be sure that all the top legs of the cross-stitches lie in the same direction. When finished with a strand of yarn, do not knot, weave in end through sts on back of afghan.

Tps (Tunisian purl stitch): Bring yarn to the front, insert hook from right to left behind the next vertical bar (same as for basic afghan stitch), yo, draw lp through. This will leave a horizontal strand of yarn across the front of the stitch. (Fig. 4) For second half of row, work off all lps on hook as in Tss.

Tks (Tunisian knit stitch): With yarn in back, insert hook from front to back bet both vertical strands of next lp, yo, and pull up a lp even with current row. (Fig. 5A and Fig. 5B, page 114) For second half of row, work off all lps on hook as in Tss.

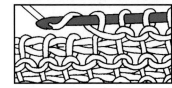

FIG. 4 Tunisian Purl Stitch

Changing colors in afghan stitch: When changing colors in the middle of a row, work across the first half of the row using the first color and pick up the required number of sts. Drop the yarn in use to the back of the work. With the second color, pick up the required number sts. Never carry a strand of yarn for more then 3 sts or 3 rows; if more than 3 or 4 sts are bet each color, beg with a new bobbin or ball of yarn. (Fig. 6A and Fig. 6B, page 114)

On the second half of the row, take the lps off the hook until 1 lp before the next color remains on the hook; drop the yarn to the back of the work. Then, with the second color, take the two different-colored lps from the hook and remove the lps in that color until 1 lp of the color remains before the next color change. Cont across the row in this manner until 1 lp remains on the hook.

WYF: With yarn in front.

FIG. 5A	FIG. 5B	FIG. 6A	FIG. 6B
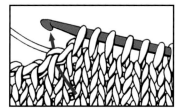		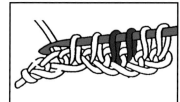	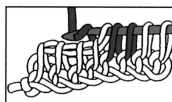

DIRECTIONS

With CA and afghan hook, ch 199 loosely.

- **Row 1:** Work in Tss Row 1 (A and B). (199 sts)
- **Row 2:** Sk first vertical bar, insert hook under next bar, yo, pull up a lp (Tss made), WYF insert hook under next bar, yo, pull up a lp (Tps made). (Tss, Tps) across ending with Tss. Rep second half of row as Row 1.
- **Row 3:** Sk first bar in this row and every first half row, Tps in next bar, (Tss, Tps) across ending with Tss in this row and every row.
- **Rows 4-21:** Rep Rows 2 and 3.
- **Row 22:** (Tss, Tps) 9 times, 161 Tss, (Tps, Tss) 9 times, Tss.
- **Row 23:** (Tps, Tss) 9 times, Tps, 159 Tss, (Tps, Tss) 10 times.
- **Rows 24-31:** Rep Rows 22 and 23.
- **Row 32:** Rep Row 22.
- **Row 33:** (Tps, Tss) 9 times, Tps, 31 Tss, (Tps, Tss) 48 times, Tps, 31 Tss, (Tps, Tss) 10 times.
- **Row 34:** (Tss, Tps) 9 times, 31 Tss, (Tps, Tss) 49 times, Tps, 31 Tss, (Tps, Tss) 9 times, Tss.
- **Rows 35-42:** Rep Rows 33 and 34.
- **Row 43:** (Tps, Tss) 9 times, Tps, 30 Tss, drop CA, with CB 3 Tks, (with CA 3 Tks, with CB 3 Tks) 16 times, with CA 30 Tss, (Tps, Tss) 10 times.

Note: When working off lps in second half of row, do color change as instructed in the Stitch Guide.

- **Row 44:** (Tss, Tps) 9 times, 31 Tss, (with CB 3 Tks, with CA 3 Tks) 16 times, with CB 3 Tks, with CA 31 Tss, (Tps, Tss) 9 times, Tss.
- **Row 45:** Rep Row 43.
- **Row 46:** (Tss, Tps) 9 times, 31 Tss, (with CA 3 Tks, with CB 3 Tks) 16 times, with CA 3 Tks, 31 Tss, (Tps, Tss) 9 times. Tss.
- **Row 47:** (Tps, Tss) 9 times, Tps, 30 Tss, (with CA 3 Tks, with CB 3 Tks) 16 times, with CA 3 Tks, 30 Tss, (Tps, Tss) 10 times.
- **Row 48:** Rep Row 46.
- **Rows 49-51:** Rep Rows 43-45.
- **Row 52:** (Tss, Tps) 9 times, 12 Tss, (Tps, Tss) 5 times, with CB 3 Tks, with CA 3 Tks, with CB 3 Tks, with CA (Tss, Tps) 49 times, Tss, with CB 3 Tks, with CA 3 Tks, with CB 3 Tks, with CA (Tps, Tss) 5 times, 12 Tss, (Tps, Tss) 9 times, Tss.
- **Row 53:** (Tps, Tss) 9 times, Tps, 12 Tss, (Tps, Tss) 4 times, Tps, with CB 3 Tks, with CA 3 Tks, with CB 3 Tks, with CA (Tps, Tss) 49 times, Tps, with CB 3 Tks, with CA 3 Tks, with CB 3 Tks, with CA (Tps, Tss) 4 times, Tps, 12 Tss, (Tps, Tss) 10 times.
- **Row 54:** Rep Row 52.

- **Row 55:** (Tps, Tss) 9 times, Tps, 12 Tss, (Tps, Tss) 4 times, Tps, 3 Tks, with CB 3 Tks, with CA 3 Tks, (Tps, Tss) 49 times, Tps, 3 Tks, with CB 3 Tks, with CA 3 Tks, (Tps, Tss) 4 times, Tps, 12 Tss, (Tps, Tss) 10 times.

- **Row 56:** (Tss, Tps) 9 times, 12 Tss, (Tps, Tss) 5 times, 3 Tks, with CB 3 Tks, with CA 3 Tks, (Tss, Tps) 49 times, Tss, 3 Tks, with CB 3 Tks, with CA 3 Tks, (Tps, Tss) 5 times, 12 Tss, (Tps, Tss) 9 times, Tss.

- **Row 57:** Rep Row 55.

- **Rows 58-60:** Rep Rows 52-54.

- **Rows 61-63:** Rep Rows 55-57.

- **Rows 64-66:** Rep Rows 52-54.

- **Rows 67-69:** Rep Rows 55-57.

- **Rows 70-72:** Rep Rows 52-54.

- **Row 73:** (Tps, Tss) 9 times, Tps, 12 Tss, (Tps, Tss) 4 times, Tps, 3 Tks, with CB 3 Tks, with CA 3 Tks, (Tps, Tss) 11 times, 56 Tss, (Tps, Tss) 10 times, Tps, 3 Tks, with CB 3 Tks, with CA 3 Tks, (Tps, Tss) 4 times, Tps, 12 Tss, (Tps, Tss) 10 times.

- **Row 74:** (Tss, Tps) 9 times, 12 Tss, (Tps, Tss) 5 times, 3 Tks, with CB 3 Tks, with CA 3 Tks, (Tss, Tps) 10 times, 59 Tss, (Tps, Tss) 10 times, 3 Tks, with CB 3 Tks, with CA 3 Tks, (Tss, Tps) 5 times, 12 Tss, (Tps, Tss) 9 times, Tss in last st.

- **Row 75:** Rep Row 73.

- **Row 76:** (Tss, Tps) 9 times, 12 Tss, (Tps, Tss) 5 times, with CB 3 Tks, with CA 3 Tks, with CB 3 Tks, with CA (Tss, Tps) 10 times, 59 Tss, (Tps, Tss) 10 times, with CB 3 Tks, with CA 3 Tks, with CB 3 Tks, with CA (Tss, Tps) 5 times, 12 Tss, (Tps, Tss) 9 times, Tss.

- **Row 77:** (Tps, Tss) 9 times, Tps, 12 Tss, (Tps, Tss) 4 times, Tps, with CB 3 Tks, with CA 3 Tks, with CB 3 Tks, with CA (Tps, Tss) 11 times, 56 Tss, (Tps, Tss) 10 times, Tps, with CB 3 Tks, with CA 3 Tks, with CB 3 Tks, with CA (Tps, Tss) 4 times, Tps, 12 Tss, (Tps, Tss) 10 times.

- **Row 78:** Rep Row 76.

- **Rows 79-81:** Rep Rows 73-75.

- **Rows 82-84:** Rep Rows 76-78.

- **Rows 85-126:** Rep Rows 73-78 seven times.

- **Rows 127-129:** Rep Rows 73-75.

- **Rows 130-147:** Rep Rows 52-57 three times.

- **Rows 148-150:** Rep Rows 52-54.

- **Rows 151-153:** Rep Rows 43-45.

- **Rows 154-156:** Rep Rows 46-48.

- **Rows 157-159:** Rep Rows 43-45.

- **Rows 160-169:** Rep Rows 34 and 33 five times.

- **Rows 170-180:** Rep Rows 22 and 23 five times. Rep Row 22 once more.

- **Rows 181-200:** Rep Rows 3 and 2. Finish off.

BORDER

- **Rnd 1:** With crochet hook and CB, begin in the lower right corner. Attach yarn with sc, 2 sc in same st, 198 sc along right edge, 3 sc in upper right

Tunisian Hearts Key

CROSS-STITCH	BACKSTITCH
S Dark Red	— Light Green
O Dark Pink	
X Country Blue	

Tunisian Hearts Center Design

Tunisian Hearts

corner, 197 sc across top, 3 sc in last st, 198 sc along left edge, 3 sc in corner, 197 sc across bottom, join with a Sl st to first sc.

■ **Rnd 2:** Work in reverse sc as follows: Ch 1, do not turn. Working from left to right, insert hook in stitch to right of hook, yo and draw yarn through, under and to the left of lp on hook, yo, draw yarn through both lps on hook (reverse sc made). Reverse sc in each sc around, 3 reverse sc in center sc of each 3-sc corner, join with a Sl st to first st, finish off.

Tunisian Hearts Border

Tunisian Hearts Key

CROSS-STITCH

S	Dark Red
O	Dark Pink
X	Country Blue

BACKSTITCH

— Light Green

Note: After stitching bottom two-thirds of afghan, rotate chart 180 degrees and stitch this section only on the top one-third of afghan.

FINISHING

Using charts, center the design on the Tunisian Stitch square and begin stitching. Stitch all vines and leaves in backstitch with one strand of Light Green yarn. Stitch all cross-stitches in color designated on chart, using double strands of yarn. For outer border embroidery, work lower two-thirds of afghan according to the charts. Then rotate charts and afghan 180 degrees to embroider top one-third. ❖

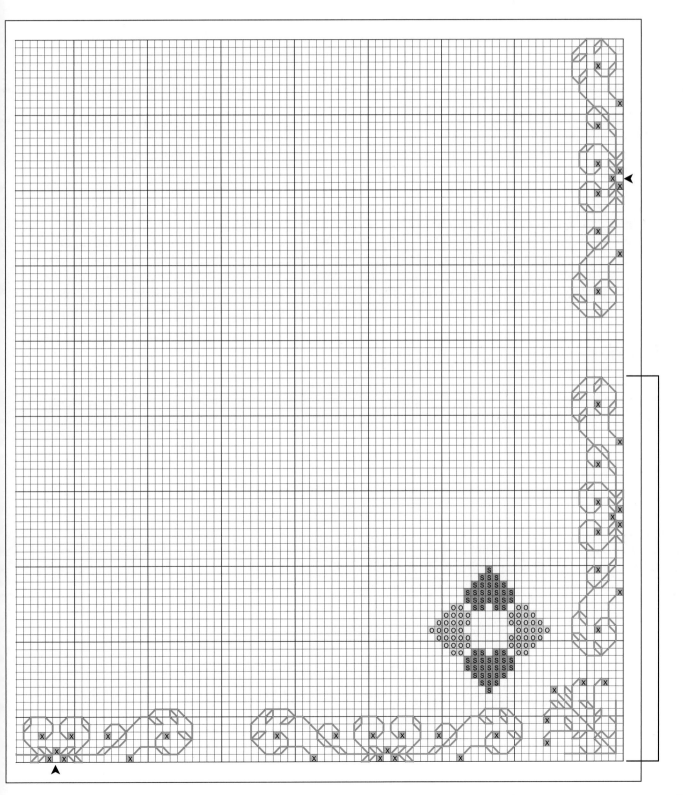

The Basics
FOR KNIT & CROCHET

GENERAL INFORMATION

GAUGE

Exact gauge is essential for your afghan to be the proper size. Gauge refers to how many stitches (or rows) there are in an inch of knitting or crocheting using a specific yarn and hook/needle size. As you begin your afghan, make a sample swatch per the individual instructions using the recommended yarn and hook/needle (a 4" swatch is usually recommended). After you complete the swatch, measure it, counting your stitches and rows carefully. If you are getting more stitches to the inch, you are working tightly and should change to a larger size hook/needle. If you are getting fewer stitches to the inch, you are working loosely and should change to a smaller size hook/needle. Keep trying until you find the hook/needle size that will give you the specified gauge. Check your gauge as you progress to ensure the correct size.

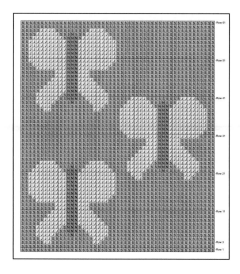

READING CHARTS

Sometimes charts (like the one above from page 88) are easier to follow than lengthy directions. Each square on the chart represents one stitch. Usually, charts are read from bottom to top, right to left for right-side rows and left to right for wrong-side rows.

WASHING INSTRUCTIONS FOR AFGHANS

MACHINE WASHING AND DRYING

Machine wash on "Gentle" or "Synthetic" setting using cool water and any detergent that does not contain bleaching agents. A small amount of fabric softener added to the final rinse will help keep your afghan soft and static-free. Machine dry at "Low" or "Perm Press" setting. Always machine dry after machine washing.

HAND WASHING AND DRYING

Wash gently in warm water using any detergent that does not contain bleaching agents. Always support the afghan during washing and rinsing and when removing the afghan from cold rinse. Bunch together and lift out in both hands. Squeeze out excess water, roll inside a towel, and squeeze again while in the towel. Spread the afghan to dry on a flat surface, shape, and allow it to dry thoroughly before moving it. Never dry an afghan in direct sunlight and never hang to dry.

DRY CLEANING

Professional dry cleaning is recommended as an alternative to automatic laundering.

Note: Always check yarn label for washing instructions.

FRINGE

1. To make a simple fringe, cut the required number of yarn lengths specified in the directions.

2. Insert a crochet hook through 1 stitch at the edge of the afghan and fold the yarn lengths in half over the hook. Pull the folded yarn partway through the stitch to form a loop. (Fig. 1)

3. Pull the yarn ends through the loop and pull tight. (Fig. 2)

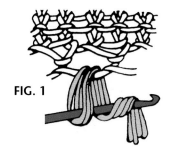

FIG. 1

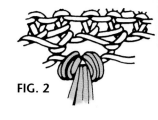

FIG. 2

STANDARD YARN WEIGHTS

Each pattern in this book provides a recommended yarn weight identified by a universal system adopted by the Yarn Council of America. Most yarn labels identify yarn weights with these symbols, making it easier to choose yarns that will work well with these afghan patterns. Look for the weight number on the universal logo when purchasing yarn for your afghans. The type of yarn and hook size will affect your gauge. Refer to the chart below for more information.

STANDARD YARN WEIGHT SYSTEM
Categories of yarn, gauge ranges, and recommended needle and hook sizes

Yarn Weight Symbol & Category Names	1 Super Fine	2 Fine	3 Light	4 Medium	5 Bulky	6 Super Bulky
Type of Yarns in Category	Sock, Fingering, Baby	Sport, Baby	DK, Light Worsted	Worsted, Afghan, Aran	Chunky, Craft, Rug	Bulky, Roving
Knit Gauge Range* in Stockinette Stitch to 4 inches	27–32 sts	23–26 sts	21–24 sts	16–20 sts	12–15 sts	6–11 sts
Recommended Needle in Metric Size Range	2.25–3.25 mm	3.25–3.75 mm	3.75–4.5 mm	4.5–5.5 mm	5.5–8 mm	8 mm and larger
Recommended Needle in U.S. Size Range	1 to 3	3 to 5	5 to 7	7 to 9	9 to 11	11 and larger
Crochet Gauge Ranges* in Single Crochet to 4 inches	21–32 sts	16–20 sts	12–17 sts	11–14 sts	8–11 sts	5–9 sts
Recommended Hook in Metric Size Range	2.25–3.5 mm	3.5–4.5 mm	4.5–5.5 mm	5.5–6.5 mm	6.5–9 mm	9 mm and larger
Recommended Hook in U.S. Size Range	B–1 to E–4	E–4 to 7	7 to I–9	I–9 to K–10½	K–10½ to M–13	M–13 and larger

* GUIDELINES ONLY: The above reflects the most commonly used gauges and needle or hook sizes for specific yarn categories.

SKILL LEVELS

Look for the skill level at the top of each project to determine the amount of experience recommended to complete the afghan. And remember, it is always good to challenge yourself! The different skill levels are defined here:

SKILL LEVEL
 **BEGINNER**

Projects for first-time knitters or crocheters using basic stitches, with minimal shaping and simple finishing.

SKILL LEVEL
 **EASY**

Projects using basic stitches, repetitive stitch patterns, and simple color changes, with simple shaping and finishing.

SKILL LEVEL
 **INTERMEDIATE**

Projects with a variety of stitches or color patterns, with mid-level shaping and finishing.

SKILL LEVEL
EXPERIENCED

Projects using advanced techniques and stitches and numerous color changes, with detailed shaping and refined finishing.

The Basics for Crochet

SLIPKNOT

Note: Diagrams show a crochet hook, but the same method is used to create a slipknot with a knitting needle.

1. Make a loop. (Fig. 1A)

2. Let the working yarn fall behind loop to form pretzel shape as shown. Insert needle or hook. (Fig. 1B)

3. Gently pull both ends of yarn to close knot. (Fig. 1C)

FIG. 1A

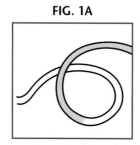

FIG. 1B

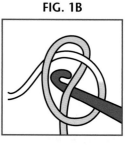

FIG. 1C

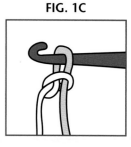

CROCHET ABBREVIATIONS

[ ] = work instructions within brackets as many times as directed

( ) = work instructions within parentheses as many times as directed

* = repeat the instructions following the single asterisk as directed

* ** = repeat instructions between single and double asterisks as many times as directed or repeat from a given set of instructions.

" = inch(es)

approx = approximately

beg = begin, beginning

bet = between

bl(s) = block(s)

BLO = back loop only

BPdc = back post double crochet

ch(s) = chain(s)

ch- = refers to chain or space previously made: e.g., ch-1 space

ch-sp = chain space

CC = contrasting color

cm = centimeter(s)

cont = continue, continuing

dc = double crochet(s)

dc2tog = double crochet 2 stitches together

dec = decrease

Fig. = figure (diagram)

FPdc = front post double crochet

FPsc = front post single crochet

FPSlst = front post slip stitch

FPtr = front post treble crochet

hdc = half double crochet(s)

inc = increase

lp(s) = loop(s)

MC = main color

mm = millimeter(s)

oz = ounce(s)

pat = pattern

pc = popcorn

rem = remaining

rep = repeat

rnd(s) = round(s)

RS = right side

sc = single crochet(s)

sc2tog = single crochet 2 stitches together

sk = skip

Sl st = slip stitch

sp(s) = space(s)

st(s) = stitch(es)

tog = together

tr = treble crochet

Tr tr = triple treble crochet

WS = wrong side

WYB = with yarn in back

WYF = with yarn in front

yd(s) = yard(s)

yo = yarn over

CROCHET HOOK SIZES

U.S.*	Metric (mm)
B-1	2.25
C-2	2.75
D-3	3.25
E-4	3.5
F-5	3.75
G-6	4.0
7	4.5
H-8	5.0
I-9	5.5

U.S.*	Metric (mm)
J-10	6.0
K-10½	6.5
L-11	8.0
M/N-13	9.0
N/P-15	10.0
P/Q	15.0
Q	16.0
S	19.0

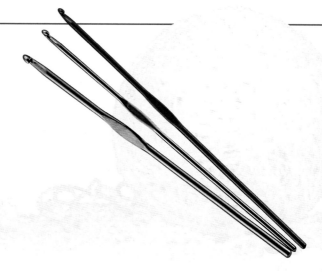

*Letter or number may vary. Rely on millimeter (mm) sizing.

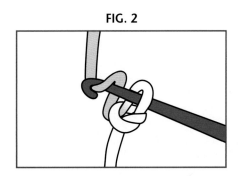

FIG. 2

CHAIN STITCH (CH)

Fig. 2: Yarn over hook and draw the yarn through to form a new loop without tightening up the previous one. Repeat to form as many chains as required. Do not count the slipknot as a chain stitch.

SLIP STITCH (SL ST)

Note: This stitch is not used on its own to produce a fabric. It is used for joining and shaping and, when needed, for carrying yarn to another part of the fabric for the next stage.

Fig. 3A: Insert the hook into the second chain from hook, yarn over, and draw the yarn through both the chain and the loop on the hook in one movement.

Fig. 3B: To join chains into a ring with a slip stitch, insert the hook into the first chain, yarn over, and draw through both the work and the yarn on the hook in one movement.

FIG. 3A

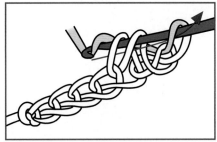

FIG. 3B

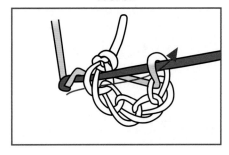

FIG. 4

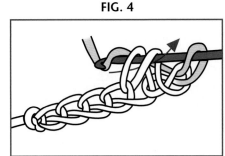
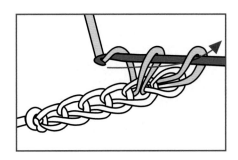

SINGLE CROCHET (SC)

Fig 4: Insert the hook into the second chain from hook. Yarn over the hook and draw the yarn through the chain only. Yarn over the hook again and draw the yarn through both loops on the hook. (one sc made)

FIG. 5

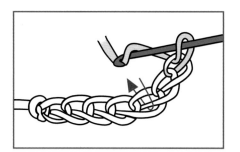 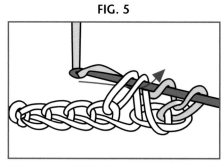 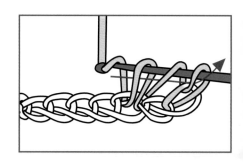

HALF DOUBLE CROCHET (HDC)

Fig. 5: Yarn over the hook and insert the hook into the third chain from the hook. Yarn over the hook and draw through the chain only. Yarn over the hook and draw through all three loops on the hook. (one hdc made)

FIG. 6

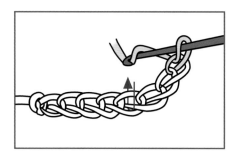 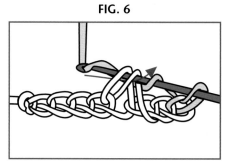 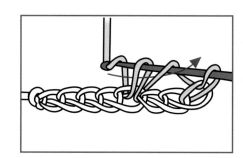

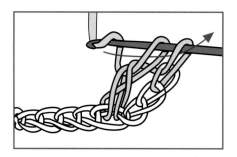 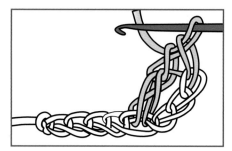

DOUBLE CROCHET (DC)

Fig. 6: Yarn over the hook and insert the hook into the fourth chain from the hook. Yarn over the hook and draw through the chain only. (Yarn over the hook and draw through 2 loops) twice. (one dc made)

FIG. 7

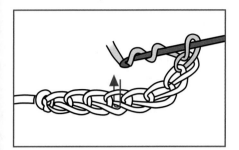 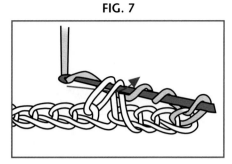 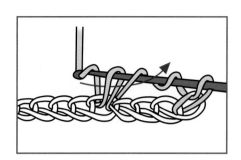

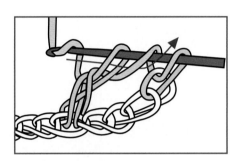 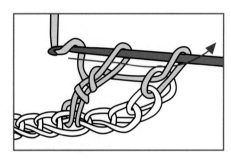

TREBLE CROCHET (TR)

Fig. 7: Yarn over the hook twice and insert the hook into the fifth chain from the hook. Yarn over the hook and draw through the chain only. Four loops are now on the hook. (Yarn over the hook and draw through 2 loops) 3 times. (one tr made)

WORKING IN BACK LOOPS ONLY (BLO)

The pattern directions will indicate when to work in the back loops. (When directions are not specific, always work under the 2 top loops of the stitches.) Working stitches in the back loops results in a ridge on the side that faces you.

When instructed to work in BLO, work in the back single strand of the stitch of the previous row. When working rows, you must tilt your work to locate the strand; when working in rounds, this strand lies along the rim of the outside edge.

FINISHING OFF

After finishing the last stitch, cut the yarn, leaving a short tail (approximately 6" long). Yarn over the hook and pull the tail through the last loop on the hook. Use the hook or a tapestry needle to draw the yarn through at least 5 stitches, winding the yarn over and under as you go.

The Basics for Knit

KNITTING ABBREVIATIONS

[ ] = work instructions within brackets as many times as directed

( ) = work instructions within parentheses as many times as directed

* = repeat the instructions following the single asterisk as directed

* ** = repeat instructions between single and double asterisks as many times as directed or repeat from a given set of instructions

" = inch(es)

approx = approximately

beg = begin, beginning

bet = between

BO = bind off

CC = contrasting color

cm = centimeter(s)

cont = continue, continuing

dec = decrease

Fig. = figure (diagram)

garter stitch = knit every row

inc = increase

k = knit

k2tog = knit 2 stitches together

k3tog = knit 3 stitches together

lp(s) = loop(s)

M1 = make one—an increase (several increases can be described as "M1")

MC = main color

mm = millimeter(s)

oz = ounce(s)

pat = pattern

p = purl

p2tog = purl 2 stitches together

p3tog = purl 3 stitches together

psso = pass slipped stitch over

rem = remaining

rep = repeat

RS = right side

sk = skip

skpo = slip, knit, pass stitch over (one stitch decreased)

sk2po = slip 1, knit 2 together, pass slipped stitch over the knit 2 together (2 stitches decreased)

sl1k = slip 1 stitch knitwise

sl2k = slip 2 stitches knitwise

sl1p = slip 1 stitch purlwise

sl2p = slip 2 stitches purlwise

Sl st = slip stitch

sp(s) = space(s)

ssk = slip, slip, knit these 2 stitches together (decrease made)

st(s) = stitch(es)

St st = stockinette stitch (knit one row; purl one row)

tog = together

WS = wrong side

WYB = with yarn in back

WYF = with yarn in front

yd(s) = yard(s)

yo = yarn over

KNITTING NEEDLE SIZES

U.S.	Metric (mm)
1	2.25
2	2.75
3	3.25
4	3.5
5	3.75
6	4.0
7	4.5
8	5.0
9	5.5
10	6.0
10½	6.5
11	8.0
13	9.0
15	10.0
17	12.75
19	15.0
35	19.0
50	25.0

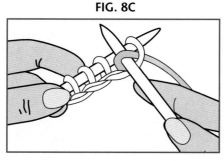

FIG. 8A

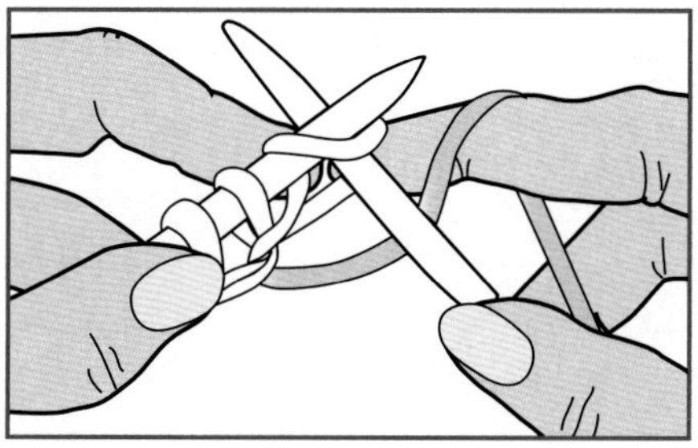

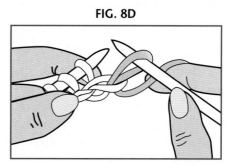

FIG. 8B

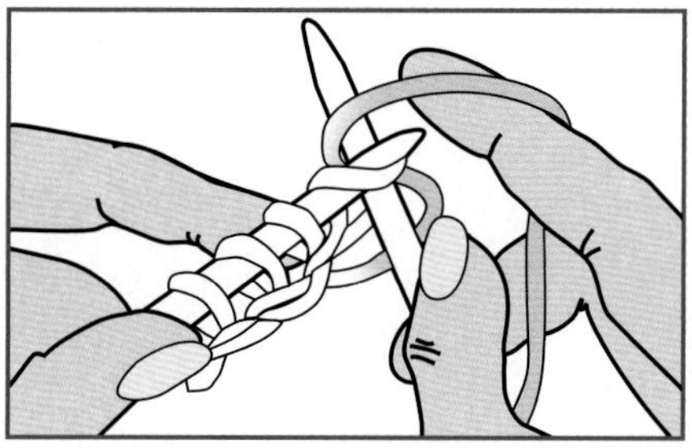

FIG. 8C

FIG. 8D

KNIT (K)

1. With yarn in back, insert the right-hand needle from front to back into the first stitch on the left-hand needle. The right-hand needle is behind the left-hand needle. (Fig. 8A)

2. Wrap the yarn around the right needle only from back to front. (Fig. 8B)

3. Pull the loop through the stitch so the loop is in front of the work. (Fig. 8C)

4. Slip the first or "old" knit stitch over and off the tip of the left-hand needle, leaving it on the right-hand needle. (Fig. 8D)

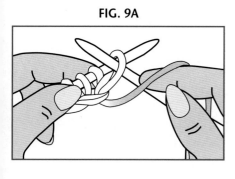

FIG. 9A

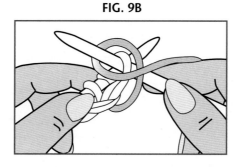

FIG. 9B

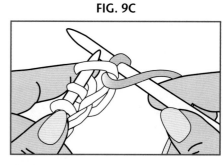

FIG. 9C

PURL (P)

1. With yarn in front of the work, insert the right-hand needle from back to front into the first stitch on the left-hand needle. (Fig. 9A)

2. Wrap the yarn on top of and around the right needle only. (Fig. 9B)

3. Keeping the working yarn firmly in your right hand, use the right needle to pull up a loop, moving backward and away from you through the stitch on the left needle. (Fig. 9C) Slip the first or "old" purl stitch over and off the tip of the left-hand needle, leaving it on the right-hand needle.

The Basics for Knit

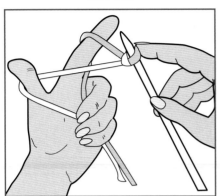 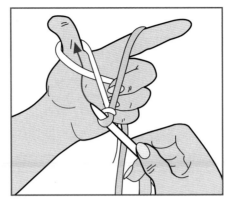 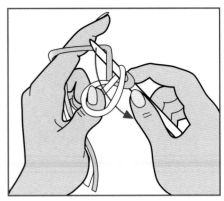

LONG TAIL CAST-ON

1. Estimate a yarn tail length that is three times the length of what the cast-on edge will be. (If you underestimate, you will have to pull out the work, add more length, and begin again.) Make a slipknot (see page 120) this distance from the yarn end and place it on the right-hand needle with the yarn tail in front and the working yarn (attached to the ball) behind the needle.

2. * Position thumb and index finger between the 2 strands of yarn. Close the other fingers into the palm of your hand and securely hold the yarn. Place the index finger of your right hand on top of the slipknot to hold it in place. (Fig. 10A)

3. Moving in an upward direction, insert the needle under the yarn on the thumb and into the loop that is formed around the thumb. (Fig. 10B) Take the needle over the top of the yarn in front of the index finger and guide it down into the thumb loop—the strand of yarn from the index finger easily moves along with the needle. (Fig. 10C) Pull the strand through the thumb loop, making a new loop on the right-hand needle.

4. Drop the yarn around the thumb and spread your index finger and thumb to tighten the loop on the needle. (one cast-on stitch made) Repeat from * to make a second cast-on stitch, and so on.

FIG. 11A   FIG. 11B   FIG. 11C

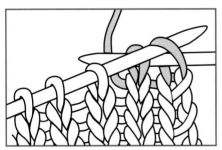 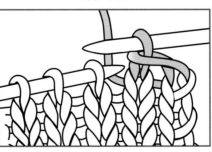 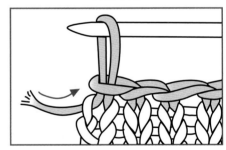

BIND OFF (BO)

Note: The diagrams shown here illustrate a knit row for the bind-off. Follow the same general technique for binding off on purl rows or if a pattern instructs you to "bind off in pattern."

1. Hold the needle with stitches in your left hand and the empty needle in your right hand. Hold the yarn in position for the knit stitch, behind your work.

2. Knit the first 2 stitches.

3. * Insert the left needle from left to right into the front loop of the first stitch on the right needle (the stitch farther from the right needle tip). (Fig. 11A)

4. Use the left needle to pull this stitch over the second stitch and drop it off the right needle. One stitch bound off; the second stitch remains on the right needle. (Fig. 11B)

5. Knit the next stitch.

6. Repeat from * until you have bound off all stitches from the left needle and one stitch remains on the right needle. Cut the yarn about 4" from the stitch and pull the yarn tail through the last stitch. (Fig. 11C) Remove the needle and pull the yarn tail to tightly.

TIP: If you tend to bind off too tightly and your bound-off edge is not as elastic as the rest of your knitting, try using a larger needle to bind off.

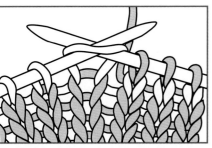

FIG. 12A

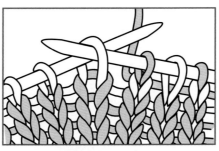

FIG. 12B

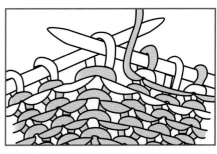

FIG. 12C

SLIP STITCH (SL ST)

When the directions instruct you to "slip a stitch," move the stitch to the right needle without knitting or purling. Always slip as if to purl unless the pattern instructions indicate otherwise, or if the stitch is part of a decrease method. A stitch that is part of a decrease is transferred to the right needle as if to knit, in the twisted position, because it will later become untwisted when the decrease is completed.

Fig. 12A: To slip as if to knit (sl1k), keep the yarn behind your work and insert the right needle into the next stitch on the left needle as if to knit it. Instead of wrapping the yarn around the needle, simply slide the stitch off the left needle and onto the right. Slipping as

if to knit transfers the stitch in a twisted position (the back loop of the stitch is now in the front). Some patterns require this, others do not.

Fig. 12B: To slip as if to purl (sl1p) with yarn in back, with the knit side facing you, insert the right needle tip into the next stitch on the left needle as if to purl, and slide the stitch onto the right needle.

Fig. 12C: To slip as if to purl with the yarn in front, with the purl side facing you, slip the stitch as if to purl. When a stitch is slipped using either of the "as if to purl" methods, the strands will not show on the knit side of the work; however, some stitch patterns reverse the normal process, so always follow instructions carefully.

YARN OVER (YO)

Fig. 13: Bring the yarn to the front of the work and then knit the following stitches as instructed. On the next row, work into the front loop of this strand (yo) as you would any other stitch, transferring it from the left needle after it is knitted.

KNIT TWO TOGETHER (K2TOG)

Fig. 14: With yarn behind your work, skip over the first stitch on the left needle and insert the right needle knitwise into the second stitch and the first (skipped-over) stitch at the same time. Knit the 2 stitches as if they were one and remove the stitches from the left needle. (one stitch decreased)

PURL TWO TOGETHER (P2TOG)

Fig. 15: With yarn in front of your work, insert the right needle through the loops of the next 2 stitches on the left needle as if to purl. Purl the 2 stitches as if they were one and remove the stitches from the left needle. (one stitch decreased)

SLIP SLIP KNIT (SSK)

Fig. 16: Slip 2 stitches knitwise, one at a time, from the left needle onto the right needle. With yarn in back, insert the left needle tip from left to right into the front loops of both slipped stitches. Knit both stitches together from this position. (one stitch decreased)

FIG. 13

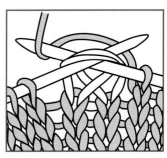

FIG. 14

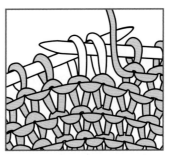

FIG. 15

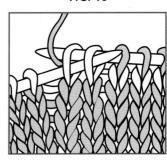

FIG. 16

The Basics for Embroidery

GETTING STARTED

Unless indicated otherwise, begin stitching at the center of the design. Every chart has arrows that indicate the horizontal and vertical centers. With your finger, trace along the grid to the point where the two centers meet. Compare a symbol at the center of the chart to the key and choose which yarn color to stitch first. To find the center of the fabric, count the stitches from the top and bottom of the area to be cross-stitched. Use one strand of yarn unless instructed otherwise and thread it into a blunt-tip needle.
Note: All embroidered afghans in this book are cross-stitched over the afghan stitch. The squares on the diagrams below represent the bars/squares formed by the afghan stitch. For additional "cross-stitch over afghan stitch" instructions, see pages 96-97.

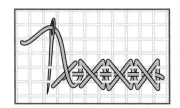

TO SECURE YARN AT THE BEGINNING

The most common way to secure the beginning tail of the yarn is to hold it under the first four or five stitches.

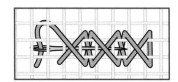

TO SECURE YARN AT THE END

To finish, slip the threaded needle under previously stitched threads on the wrong side of the fabric for four or five stitches, weaving the yarn back and forth a few times. Clip the yarn.

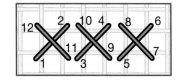

CROSS-STITCH OVER AFGHAN STITCH

Cross-stitch over afghan stitch is worked from a chart with a key for the symbols and colors used. Each square on chart represents one bar. One cross-stitch is worked over one vertical bar. To work cross-stitch, count over required number of bars to where you wish to begin. Bring yarn through from back of work to

front, leaving 2" end to be worked over (do not knot). Work cross-stitches as shown, being careful not to pull stitches too tightly. Be sure that all the top legs of the cross-stitches lie in the same direction. When finished with a strand of yarn, do not knot, weave in end through sts on back of afghan.

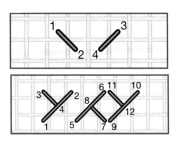

QUARTER AND THREE-QUARTER CROSS-STITCHES

To obtain rounded shapes in a design, use quarter and three-quarter cross-stitches. To make quarter cross-stitches estimate the center of the square. Three-quarter cross-stitches combine a quarter cross-stitch with a half cross-stitch. Both stitches may slant in any direction.

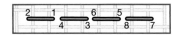

BACKSTITCHES

Backstitches define and outline the shapes of a design. For most projects, backstitches require only one strand of yarn.

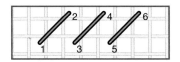

HALF CROSS-STITCHES

A half cross-stitch is a single diagonal or half a cross-stitch. They are indicated on the chart by a diagonal colored symbol.

STEM STITCH

Stem stitches are used for outlines and fine lines. Working from left to right, take regular small stitches along the line indicated on the chart. The thread always emerges on the left side of the previous stitch. ❖